Latin-*ish*

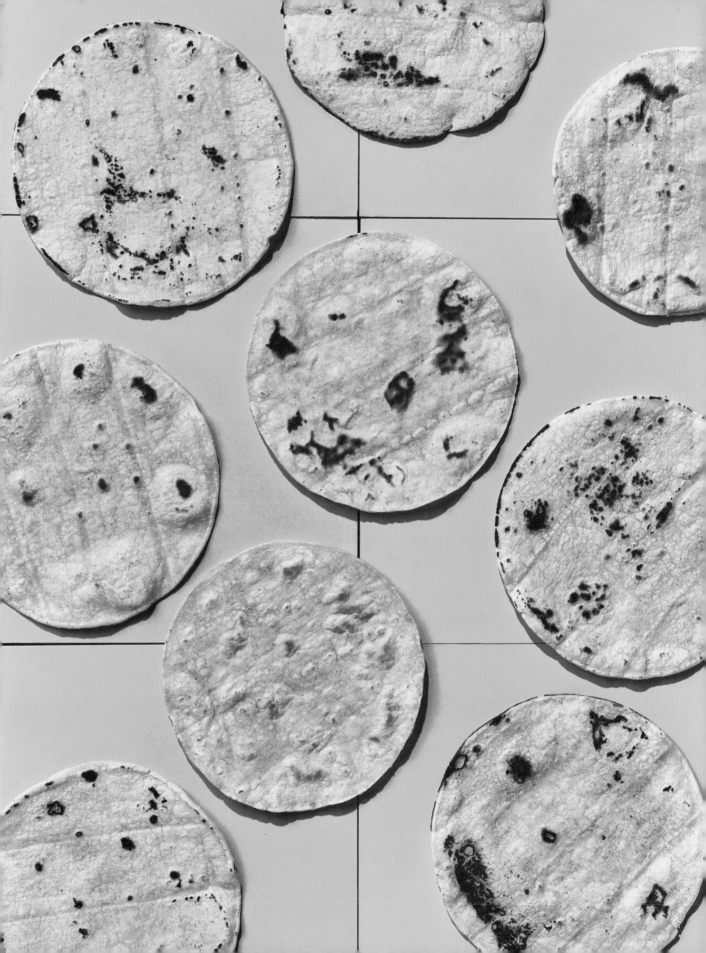

Latin-*ish*

More Than 100 Recipes Celebrating American Latino Cuisines

Marisel Salazar
Photography by Hipolito Torres

Countryman Press

An Imprint of W. W. Norton & Company
Independent Publishers Since 1923

For information about permission to reproduce selections from this book, write to
Permissions, Countryman Press, 500 Fifth Avenue, New York, NY 10110

For information about special discounts for bulk purchases, please contact
W. W. Norton Special Sales at specialsales@wwnorton.com or 800-233-4830

Manufacturing by Toppan Leefung Pte. Lte.
Book design by Allison Chi
Production manager: Devon Zahn

Countryman Press
www.countrymanpress.com

An imprint of W. W. Norton & Company, Inc.
500 Fifth Avenue, New York, NY 10110
www.wwnorton.com

978-1-68268-826-7

10 9 8 7 6 5 4 3 2 1

To my sister, Marisabel, who took care of me during one of the most significant periods of my life, which happened while I was writing this book, and who has been my protector and big sister always, no matter how old I get. I'm so lucky to have you as my sister.

To my nieces, Livia and Sofia, who bring a smile to my face. I hope your tía makes you proud. I love you girls so much.

To my brother-in-law, Michael, who has been just like a brother. Thank you for putting up with me.

To my resilient mother, Maria, who has served as both mother and father for my whole life. I love you.

To San Antonio, Texas, which took me in as one of its own and helped me heal.

Contents

Introducti

on

My heritage is Cuban, Panamanian, and Peruvian. Part of my family fled Cuba, and I was born in Panama City. I don't know my biological father, but my mother later married a man serving in the US Navy, and his job took us around the world. After Panama, I lived in Hawaii, Japan, Virginia, New York, and Madrid—all before I turned 21 years old. Because I've lived in and visited so many countries, I have less of a longing for living in the past.

I embrace novelty and change because that's all I've known. My food adventures, undertaken fearlessly and without judgment, include eating tripe swimming in tomato sauce, slurping starchy gray-purple poi, and swallowing natto, just for starters. Not having preconceived notions sounds like the ultimate freedom, but I grew up believing that burritos were American. By the end of this cookbook, hopefully you'll agree.

Welcome to My Table

My maternal grandmother, Isabel, a dancer and showgirl, grew up in Havana. As a child, I grew up eating Latino dishes that passed from her, through my mother, Maria, to me. My mother made meals in her best Julia Child, Jacques Pépin, and Martha Stewart modes for my sister and me. A single parent, she made sure that we experienced all kinds of cuisines and recipes sourced from the greats through their cookbooks. Even in Hawaii and Japan, we ate Cuban and Panamanian food, replicating family recipes as best we could. Can you imagine making *ropa vieja*, a classic Cuban dish, using ingredients found only in Japan? I can, and I recommend the adventure!

Being a third-culture kid (page 55) gave me a unique view of American cuisines. My travels introduced me to Americans from almost every part of the country. If New York City, where I live now, serves as a melting pot for the world, military bases abroad do the same for Americans from all states and territories.

My mother says that I love to suffer. I've never taken the easy way, not that I often had that choice. But one of the ways that I do love to suffer is as a writer. When younger, I contemplated a career as a news journalist, cherishing the idea of becoming the next Christiane Amanpour. After all, "food writer" rarely qualifies as desirable or even possible for children of single mothers. When I was in college, food writing didn't have a road map in the way that it (maybe) does now, and fancy unpaid internships at good magazines in New York City cost money. But in 2010, an anchovy-stuffed olive in Madrid changed my life. At the Mercado de San Miguel, that salty, savory mouthful completely floored me. Fireworks exploded from my mouth to the rest of my body. My culinary awakening tasted . . . *sublime*. That exquisite burst of flavors might have sent others on a simple quest: "Can I buy more of these? How many can I carry through airport security and customs?" But my mind leapt straight to forensics: *How did this come together? What's the story, the process? What history and events led to this perfect moment in my mouth?* That unexpected encounter inspired my calling to become a food writer, recipe developer, and television host. But getting there required a lot of hard work.

My postcollege, entry-level day jobs in Washington, DC, afforded me the necessary leeway to pursue small kitchen externships, while moonlighting as a food writer gave my life the spice that I craved. In 2014, a blessing-in-disguise layoff encouraged me to put all my eggs in the NYC basket, which allowed me to diversify my culinary experience by copywriting and starting a clandestine granola business (page 23), selling wholesale to boutique hotels in SoHo and Nolita. By day, I interviewed chefs, and my nights overflowed with baking for my business and researching. The more I wrote about food, the more people learned my name and the more chefs I met. Editors commissioned me to write for them, to develop stories and recipes for Latin American dishes and other cuisines. Then producers reached out to book me as an on-camera expert and host, which has helped my work reach millions of eyeballs. That work often explores large, ambitious topics, as does this book, which surveys the history and recipes of American Latino cuisines as a full gastronomic ecosystem.

Welcome to My Cookbook

Many cookbook authors celebrate the traditional cuisine of their immigrant families, but my experience as a multicultural immigrant has inspired me to look at how migration shapes food beyond just my own family's history. After all, America is a country of immigrants, so we all have embraced cuisines from other cultures on a vast scale. Yes, you'll find some recipes from my experience and my family, but by tracing the evolution of Latino cuisines in this country, you also will find recipes from your family and heritage.

For many people, particularly first-generation Americans, food serves as an easy way to revisit a cherished time or place or as an introduction to somewhere new or unknown. It can feel tempting to romanticize the past, to embrace the belief that older or more traditional means better or more authentic. Some of us fantasize about how our ancestors or predecessors ate, ignoring or repressing that, over time, food changes for lots of reasons, including geopolitics, science, trends, availabilities, and plain old happy accidents. But I'm not a historical reenactor. Recipes change because, over time, locations, circumstances, ingredients, and people change. That's how food culture evolves, and I love it.

In America, tacos have become as mainstream as apple pie. Tortillas outsell hamburger buns, tortilla chips outsell potato chips, and salsa outsells ketchup. Mexican food consistently ranks in the country's top three cuisines. This cookbook aims to desegregate the arbitrary, lingering divide between Latino and American foods because American Latino cuisines *are* American food—in exactly the same way that American hamburgers aren't German and American pizza isn't Italian. As immigrants or their descendants, we assimilate, change, and evolve. We hold onto our heritage, yes, but we actively absorb aspects of other cultures. New Englanders aren't English anymore, and New Mexicans aren't Mexican anymore. No matter where we or our families came from, we're Americans. So, you're not holding a Latino cookbook full of Latino dishes; you're holding an American cookbook full of American recipes for everyone to make and enjoy.

A Taste of History

The roots of Latin American and American Latino cuisines stretch back to pre-European Indigenous foods. Many plants that we know and love originated in the Western Hemisphere: avocado, cacao, cashew, chile pepper, corn, epazote, guava, papaya, passion fruit, peanut, pecan, pineapple, potato, pumpkin and squash, tomato and tomatillo, vanilla, and more. Before Europeans arrived, Native Americans had domesticated countless varieties, innovating cultivars of beans, corn, squashes, and other plants. About 60 percent of the world's food supply today originated in North America alone.

The Great Dying, the unimaginable loss of up to 90 percent of Native Americans by diseases introduced by Europeans, devastated the rich, expansive cultures of the Western Hemisphere. As a result, we have few exclusively Indigenous dishes now, but many words for plants or ingredients survive, particularly from Nahuatl, the language of the Aztecs: *Ahuacatl* became avocado; *chilli* varies in spelling but means "chile," as in the pepper; *chilpoctli* (chile + smoke) gave us chipotle. From Nahautl, Mayan, or both, *chocolatl* became chocolate, and Taíno, spoken by the peoples of the Caribbean, gave us the place name Daiquirí. In Nahuatl, *ízquitl* means "toasted corn," giving us *esquites*; *mexcalli* means "cooked agave" and became mezcal. Like chilli, *molli* varied to mole and means "sauce." *Xitomatl* and *xicamatl* became tomato and jicama. Perhaps the relative simplicity of the few truly Indigenous dishes that do survive allowed them to persevere as Native peoples endured disease, enslavement, forced migration, genocide, war, and other cataclysms of colonization. Those foods include chi-

laquiles, corn pone, fry bread, tamales, and tortillas, many of which you'll find in this collection.

The other major foundation of American Latino food comes, of course, from Europe, beginning in antiquity with the Romans, who began their conquest of Iberia in 220 BC. From those ancient days, we have quince paste—*membrillo* in Spanish, *marmelada* in Portuguese—which gave us marmalade. We know "Roman bread" as French toast now, and the ancient Romans loved deviled eggs.

After the dissolution of the Roman Empire, the Muslim conquest arose in the Arabian peninsula and wrapped around three sides of the Mediterranean. With the spread of Islam, rice and *horchata* came from North Africa to al-Andalus, the province of the Umayyad Caliphate that covered most of Iberia. From Southeast Asia, Islamic trade routes brought bananas, oranges, and other foods to Europe.

Then everything changed in 1492. On January 2, the Reconquista—the centuries-long military campaign to eliminate Muslim control of Iberian lands—came to an end with the fall of the Emirate of Granada to Queen Isabel I of Castile. On March 31, she and her husband, King Fernando II of Aragon, issued the Alhambra Decree, expelling all Jews from the two kingdoms and with them their culinary traditions, such as fried fish. On August 3, Cristoforo Colombo (Christopher Columbus), seeking a new trade route to Asia for its precious spices and other goods, sailed into the Atlantic, bringing the Age of Exploration and European colonization to the Western Hemisphere.

The Spanish and Portuguese Empires literally changed the face of the globe. In the west, the Viceroyalty of New Spain stretched north to what today is the Canadian-American border, and the Viceroyalty of Peru extended south to Cape Horn. In the east, the Spanish crown controlled the Philippines and other islands thousands of miles into the Pacific Ocean. The Portuguese colonized almost half of South America and established numerous coastal settlements in Africa, the Middle East, and Asia. Long before the *Mayflower* Pilgrims feasted with the Wampanoag people in Plymouth Colony, Iberian explorers, missionaries, and settlers were exchanging ingredients and foodways with Indigenous peoples of the New World. In the 1500s, when the conquistadores came, they brought their own crops, livestock, disease, technology, languages, religion, and culture. With them came almonds, bananas, coffee, figs, olives, oranges, rice, sugar, and wheat. They introduced large-scale agricultural practices and livestock, such as chicken, cows, donkeys, goats, horses, and pigs. Some of America's largest agricultural industries began with foods that the Spanish brought to North America: citrus and nut orchards in Florida and the Southwest, cattle ranches in Texas, wineries in California.

The Native peoples who survived the double-barreled onslaught of disease and colonization adapted their own cooking traditions, using new foods and culinary techniques, such as making cheese and rice dishes inspired by paella, baking with wheat, and drinking wine and using it as a cooking ingredient.

Migration and Authenticity

As one of the major themes of this book, diaspora affects numerous peoples, both willing and involuntary. The Spanish and Portuguese shipped their culinary traditions to the rest of the world, but after that the migration of peoples, ingredients, and dishes flows in multiple directions and often in surprising ways.

Hernando Cortés de Monroy y Pizarro Altamirano, who conquered the Aztec Empire, brought tomatoes to northwest Africa in the mid-1500s, which, over time, led to the development of shakshuka (page 26). The transatlantic slave trade forced enslaved people from West Africa to the Americas, and, starting around 1760, the Highland Clearances also brought

Scots, albeit in starkly different circumstances. From the convergence of those peoples, southern fried chicken (page 93) eventually emerged. From South America, the Spanish brought the first pineapple to Hawaii in 1813. A few decades later, King Kamehameha III invited ranch hands from Spanish California to teach Hawaiians how to handle cattle. Italians settled in large numbers in Argentina and Brazil, and spaghetti (page 59) came to the Dominican Republic with Italian migration in the late 1800s.

In 1900, a hurricane devastated the sugar industry in Puerto Rico, after which the Hawaiian Sugar Planters' Association invited thousands of Puerto Ricans to the Pacific to work. In the 1940s, the emigration of Jews from Syria to Panama introduced muhammara (page 7) to Central America. Fish tacos (page 69) arose in Baja California in the 1950s and traveled north into Alta California. In that decade and the next, North African Jews brought shakshuka to Israel, New York City, and beyond. Cuban pizza (page 112), which may have originated with Italian immigrants in the 1930s, traveled from the island nation to Miami in the 1980s. In 1994, the North American Free Trade Agreement increased cross-cultural exchange between America and Mexico, leading to the ascendance of guacamole (pages 200–203) and the creation of Philly Cheesesteak Quesadillas (page 100).

In Los Angeles, mole followed in the 1990s footsteps of carne asada and joined forces with French fries (page 78)—which already had made their way into burritos in San Diego (page 75)—to create the Latino equivalent of poutine in the early 2000s. Also in Los Angeles, the prevalence of Mexicans working in Koreatown kitchens (page 72) led to the tasty confluence of those two cuisines.

All of which brings us to the issue of authenticity. An Italian Spanish immigrant created *pan Cubano* in Florida, but does that origin make it less Cuban? An American engineer in Cuba invented the *Daiquirí* (page 172), and the Catalonia-born owner of the leg-

endary Havana bar that popularized it made a frozen version (page 173). It's a Cuban cocktail, for sure, but is one version more authentic than the other? A Mexican restaurateur invented nachos (page 42) for Americans who had crossed the border and wanted something new for lunch. The 1940s origin stories for chimichangas (page 104) take place in Mexican restaurants in Arizona, so does that make the dish Mexican or American? After the Communist Revolution, Miami popularized the Cuban Sandwich (page 82), which doesn't exist in Cuba, so is it really Cuban? In 1950, a Mexican man in Manhattan received a patent for a machine to make hard-shell tacos (page 61). In San Bernadino, Glen Bell Jr. copied the food of a neighboring Mexican café (page 61) and, in the racially separated 1960s, introduced many white Americans to Mexican food. A Mexican restaurateur in Dallas invented a frozen margarita machine (page 185), so does that make a frozen margarita any less authentic than a regular margarita? Mexicans who moved to San Diego put French fries in a burrito in the 1980s. In San Francisco, the Mission burrito, which had emerged at one Mexican restaurant or another in San Francisco in the 1960s, became the style that, in 1993, the first Chipotle restaurant directly copied (page 85) when it opened in Denver. Does chain popularity make that style any less valid? A Puerto Rican in Chicago Americanized a Caribbean plantain sandwich (page 106), which people in Puerto Rico then started eating, but does its Windy City origin make it less legitimate? What determines authenticity, a place, a person, or something else? In America—a mixing, melting pot of cultures—the question of authenticity never ends. I should know.

COMMUNIST ICE CREAM AND A QUESTIONABLE BURRITO

If you've eaten at a Cuban restaurant or ever set foot in South Florida, you probably have seen the Cuban sandwich on a menu: a combination of juicy pork, Swiss cheese, pickles, and mustard on Cuban bread. But that sandwich originated in a cigar factory town

that merged with Tampa, Florida. My family, part of which hails from Havana, had never encountered the sandwich until coming to the United States. But we ate it as easily and happily as we embraced our new identities as Cuban Panamanian Americans. I always have embraced being Latina and American. Others haven't been so inclusive or forward-thinking.

For "real" Americans, I've never been American *enough*, and I've never been Latina *enough* for "real" Latinos. In my early 20s, I traveled to Cuba to meet my long-lost *tías abuelas* (great-aunts). More than 80 years old, they took the bus from La Lisa, a working-class neighborhood on the outskirts of Havana, to see me. They wept as they hugged me, a blood embodiment of my maternal grandmother, Abuela Isabel, who fled the island as a young woman.

"You are the closest thing to touching our sister," they said, crying.

At the famous, state-run Heladería Coppelia—a grandiose, must-visit ice cream parlor—we waited in line for frozen delights. My tías abuelas bubbled with excitement to share this most Cuban of establishments with me. We ordered an *ensalada*, a five-scoop bowl, and licked the rapidly melting cream in the park. The bittersweet experience felt almost uncomfortable. They so desperately wanted to show whatever hospitality they could afford, and instantly we embraced one another fully as family. They gave me a framed photo of my grandmother, who looked like a beautiful Virgin Mary with a sad look in her eyes. I gave them Ferrero Rocher chocolates, soap, toilet paper, and American dollars.

But during that trip, other islanders flatly rejected my Cubanity, as I like to call it. One balmy, humid night, some friends and I were walking along El Malecón. Dark ocean waves crashed onto the sea wall, and we squealed, laughing, as we tried to avoid the spray. Other *jóvenes* (teens and young adults) had flooded the esplanade, dancing to music from handheld radios, drinking Cristal, a Cuban beer, and smoking. My friends and I shimmied over to a group blaring timba, and we danced with them. The dancing slowed into conversation, and we shared that, having come from America, we were fellow Cubans visiting family on the island.

"You're not Cuban," they said.

"Of course we're Cuban. We have family here, and our families came from here before escaping to the USA," we explained.

They grew visibly, audibly irritated. "But they left, and you live there. You're American. You're no longer Cuban."

The conversation took place entirely in Spanish, so when had I lost my Cuban card? Was it when I became an American citizen? Did being American override and exclude all other identities? I didn't think so, but those Habaneros certainly did.

Whenever someone asks what I think of Cuban food, my stomach hurts. Stifled by years of authoritarian control, Cuban cuisine hasn't changed or evolved. The island has no Michelin stars or World's 50 Best Restaurants. When I was visiting and staying in *casas particulares* (homestays), the humble food often came from poor-quality ingredients because most people didn't have access to or the money for better. A month after my visit, when my tías abuelas passed away, another irreplaceable link to the past broke, but what was there to romanticize about that past?

As a food writer and critic, I often hear surprising dismissals about certain American Latino dishes. "Oh, that's not *real* Mexican food," culinary colleagues proclaim proudly, snubbing some new fast-casual Tex-Mex place. But their holier-than-thou attitudes contrast starkly with their empty plates that, for mere moments, held warm chips and queso or zesty chili con carne and cornbread.

"Of course not," I reply, dumbfounded. "This is American food, not Latin American food."

How could they not see this unique gastronomy on its own terms? With roots both American and Latino,

it has spread across the world. In Helsinki, while shopping at the S-Mart supermarket chain and wandering the prepared-food aisles, I spotted a "Tex-Mex Salad Kit"—in *Finland* of all places!

My mother's second husband was a naval officer from Denver whose job took us to military bases in the Pacific before we moved to America. As a result, I grew up with two different kinds of Latino food: the traditional version from Latin America and the American version. My mother shared traditional dishes from Cuba, Panama, and other countries, while Husband #2 and other Americans abroad made Breakfast Tacos (page 13), Cuban Sandwiches (page 82), Loaded Nachos (page 105), Mexican Casserole (page 114), New Orleans Hot Tamales (page 96), Texas Chili con Carne (page 91), an endless list of burritos specific to states and even cities, and so much more. The story for each of those dishes always began: "Well, back home in America, in [State], we make this." Not once did anyone call those foods traditional, Latin American, or Hispanic—because they're American.

Case in point: the Colorado Burrito (page 55). While we were living in Japan, Husband #2 ordered flour tortillas and canned green chile sauce—available at the time only in the Midwest and adjacent states—to make that dish. The cuisines of Mexico's northern highlands, where wheat grows, use flour tortillas, but most Mexican tortillas consist of corn. That canned green goo didn't come from Mexico, but neither did the burrito. It came from Colorado. It's not Latin American, it's American Latino.

Necessity Invents Variation

Many of the dishes in this collection developed as they did for the simple reason of adaptation, another major theme of the book. Most variations of *torrejas* (page 2) use stale bread in the same way that *chilaquiles* (page 24) repurpose stale tortillas. Horchata starts with barley in North Africa, changes to tiger nuts in Spain, shifts to rice or almonds in Mexico, incorporates dairy milk in Texas, and involves other ingredients elsewhere, all depending on what's available (page 192). We have records of the different tamales that the Aztecs ate, and today every country in Latin America makes them differently, as do certain American states. The Aztecs also ate chile stew, to which the Spanish added beef, which later turned into something like bouillon bricks for a cowboy field stew that became Texas Chili con Carne (page 91).

Cubans in Tampa made use of ingredients available from their Italian neighbors, adding Genoa salami to their Cuban Sandwiches (page 82). *Migas* (page 16) vary widely from San Antonio to Mexico City, but both versions make use of kitchen crumbs, whether actual or metaphorical. New Orleans Hot Tamales (page 96) skip the corn husks and use cornmeal in the filling instead of nixtamalized masa harina in a surrounding dough. An Irish bartender in Tijuana updated the daisy cocktail with readily available Tequila, creating the crowd-favorite margarita (page 170). Italians brought spaghetti to the Caribbean, and, when it cost less than other ingredients, Dominicans adopted and transformed it into a new dish (page 59).

Fajitas (page 124) became popular because they allowed restaurants to profit from a cheap, unwanted cut of beef. We have dedicated frozen margarita machines (page 185) because 7-Eleven wouldn't sell a Slurpee machine to an enterprising restaurant owner. A pizza-chain owner didn't want a franchise to sell tacos, so, splitting the difference, he invented Taco Pizza (page 63). A stadium concession company created shelf-stable liquid cheese to save time and sell more nachos (page 105). Fed up with bottom-shelf liquors and frozen concentrates or boxed juices, bartenders rediscovered the importance of quality ingredi-

ents and juicing citrus fresh, which led to the craft cocktail renaissance.

All those forces at work behind the scenes of the recipes in this book explain why and how cuisines grow, change, and evolve, expanding our palate and mind.

Countries and Cuisines

We've had a wide-ranging history lesson, so let's cover our bases with some geography. Latin America consists of Argentina, Bolivia, Brazil, Chile, Colombia, Costa Rica, Cuba, the Dominican Republic, Ecuador, Guatemala, Honduras, Mexico, Nicaragua, Panama, Paraguay, Peru, (Puerto Rico), El Salvador, Uruguay, and Venezuela, and, yes, we need to address a few points in that list.

This cookbook is called *Latin-ish*—not *Hispan-ish*—because it includes American foods that originated in Brazil, formerly part of the Portuguese Empire. Broadly, "Latin" America *should* denote any land in the Western Hemisphere once ruled by a European country with a language that developed from Latin, so Spanish, Portuguese, *and* French. But in practice, when talking about Latin America, no one means French Guiana, Guadeloupe, Haiti, Louisiana, Martinique, Quebec, Saint Barthélemy, Saint Martin, and so on. "Iberian America" technically would be accurate, but it's a mouthful and no one uses it (or wants to). Also, Puerto Rico appears in parentheses because it's an organized territory of the United States, not a sovereign nation, but—as with most of the rest of the countries in the list—the island belonged to the Spanish crown for almost 400 years, so parenthetically it belongs.

Those countries give us our starting point, but, again, this isn't a Latin American cookbook. It's a collection of dishes that people—who came, or whose families came, from those countries to America—eat here now. That broad category divides roughly into

seven distinct cuisines: Tex-Mex, Southwest, Cal-Mex, Floribbean, Latino Southern, NYC Latino, and Midwest Latino.

In other countries, stringent laws regulate the authenticity and quality of breads, butters, cheeses, honey, meats, oils, spirits, vinegars, wine styles, and much more, down to specific ingredients and even amounts. America has few protected designations of origin or geographic indications: American viticultural areas for wine regions, Bourbon, Florida oranges, Idaho potatoes, Vidalia onions, Washington State apples, and that's pretty much it. So these culinary traditions have blurry boundaries and rough edges. With that in mind, let's take a closer look.

TEX-MEX

Tex-Mex is Mexican food, but most people don't think of it that way. Remember, Texas belonged to New Spain for 130 years and became a province of Mexico for 15 before seceding in 1836. (After that, it existed as an independent country for nine years before joining America.) That history matters because "Tex-Mex" mostly refers to the cooking of Mexicans living in Texas. The cuisine blends Indigenous, Spanish, Mexican, and German traditions.

In the 1500s, conquistadores introduced wheat and cattle to the area, and cumin came from Morocco by way of the Canary Islands to San Antonio, the birthplace of Tex-Mex. The hyphen appeared in the 1920s, when the phrase described Tejanos, meaning Americans of Mexican descent who lived in Texas. Later, it shifted to describe the food. From 1830 to 1900, many German immigrants settled in the state, particularly in and around San Antonio. They founded Boerne, Fredericksburg, New Braunfels, and other towns and contributed to culinary traditions and the culture at large. German butchers helped establish Texas barbecue, and a German immigrant created Tampico Dust, the first commercial chili powder. Largely avoiding seafood, the German influence on Tex-Mex makes

heavy use of black olives, Cheddar cheese, Flour Tortillas (page 215), ground beef, Refried Beans (page 230), sour cream, and Taco Seasoning (page 198) in dishes often fried or baked. That influence helped pioneer Breakfast Tacos (page 13), Texas Chili con Carne (page 91), and other dishes.

SOUTHWESTERN

New Mexico and Arizona always count as southwestern, but surrounding states—Texas, Oklahoma, Colorado, Utah, Nevada, and California—sometimes do and sometimes don't. The Sonoran Desert covers a significant portion of Arizona, so some people call the Grand Canyon State's subset of the tradition Sonoran.

Chiles and sauces made from them take center stage. Beans, corn, and squash, the "three sisters," figure prominently as well, specifically pinto beans, blue heritage corn, and *calabacitas* (summer squash). Southwest cooking tends to use more beef and pork. Blending Navajo, Hopi, and Pueblo traditions with Mexican and European, it overlaps somewhat with Tex-Mex, but smothering foods in red and green chile sauce is emblematic, as is more plant-based cuisine.

CAL-MEX

A Mexican province until the Treaty of Guadalupe Hidalgo ended the Mexican-American War, California has many Latino dishes specific to individual cities, from San Diego and Los Angeles to San Francisco and Sausalito. Cal-Mex blends native ingredients, traditional Mexican cooking, and progressive, modern culinary techniques. It features an abundance of coastal seafood, black or white beans, shredded meat rather than ground, extensive use of the native Hass avocado, corn tortillas rather than flour, lighter Mexican-style cheeses and *cremas*, a preference for fresh or grilled foods rather than fried, and plenty of vegetables. Cal-Mex focuses on plant-forward seasonality, but it also gave rise to Cheetos, Fritos, and

Doritos; Korean-Mexican food and Mexican teriyaki bowls; massive Mission Burritos (page 85), steak ranchero taco trucks, and more.

Alta California

Chicano chefs in Southern California developed this regional cuisine that blends classic culinary techniques and (usually) elevated tacos. It began with Wes Avila of Guerrilla Tacos, Ray Garcia of Broken Spanish, Eduardo Ruiz of Corazon y Miel, and Carlos Salgado of Taco María. The heirloom Mexican corn tortilla serves as the cuisine's foundation, but other signature dishes include duck with date-sweetened mole, Mole Fries (page 78), and *uni* tuna tostadas. With a focus on high-quality California produce and ingredients, it aims to preserve cultural heritage while pushing southern Cal-Mex cuisine forward. Think of it as Chicano gastronomy.

FLORIBBEAN

The roots of this cuisine begin with the arrival of the Spanish in the 1500s, but it developed its characteristic identity as waves of Caribbean, Hispanic, Italian, and Chinese immigrants came to Florida in the late 1800s. After the Communist Revolution of 1959, it kicked into overdrive with a large influx of Cubans, followed by other Caribbean migrations. In the 1980s, the work of the Mango Gang—chiefly Norman van Aken, Mark Militello, Douglas Rodriguez, and Allen Susser—helped formalize and promote the style. Also called New Era cuisine, it takes inspiration from Bahamian, Cuban, and Jamaican traditions and takes advantage of Caribbean foods that grow in South Florida, such as malanga, palmetto, and yuca. Seafood plays a major role, as do regional fruits, including Key lime, mango, and pineapple. Floribbean dishes include arroz con pollo, blackened grouper, conch fritters, the Cuban Sandwich (page 82), Haitian *griot*, Jamaican jerk chicken, Key lime pie, and swamp cabbage (hearts of palm salad).

LATINO SOUTHERN

That header may not be the best term for encompassing the various Latino cuisines that have woven into the South. Perhaps, from the Southern Foodways Alliance, the Latino South (El Sur Latino) works better. Whatever the name, Mexican food helped bring the other cuisines to the region. Both cultures understand and cherish comfort food and eating economically. They embrace beans and rice, barbecue/*barbacoa*, pulled pork/*pastor*, and making use of tripe, tongue, and other offal. In the 1930s, Juan "Big John" Mora, an illegal immigrant from Mexico, created the pig ear sandwich—boiled pigs' ears, slaw, vinegar, mustard, and Mexican hot sauce in a bun—in his restaurant in Jackson, Mississippi.

Arroz con pollo has become so popular that it goes by its acronym, ACP, on some menus in the South. Many Latin American countries have a version of the chicken-and-rice dish, particularly Cuba; also Puerto Rico. It ended up in Dixieland because, though not a Mexican dish, Mexican restaurants there served it. But then it changed. Depending on the source country, traditional arroz con pollo consists of tomato or saffron rice cooked in one pot with chicken, pimientos, olives, and peas. In the South, it has become plain rice with grilled chicken breast and cheese sauce, and Southerners *love* it.

Some folks use tomatillos in fried green tomatoes and Jalapeño peppers in their savory grits or cornbread. "Carne asada tacos are now as southern as biscuits and gravy," notes food writer Gustavo Arellano. Soul-Mex or Sur Latino dishes also include Arkansas Delta Tamales (page 121), Collard Greens Empanadas (page 66), Latino Fried Chicken (page 93), and New Orleans Hot Tamales (page 96).

NYC LATINO

Latino people make up almost 30 percent of New York City's population. The City That Never Sleeps has large, established Puerto Rican, Dominican,

and Mexican communities and sizable numbers of Ecuadorians, Salvadorans, and Colombians. Afro-Caribbean and Chinese-Cuban migrants also helped launch the soul food movement of the 1960s and '70s.

Nuyorican and Caribbean
New York City has the largest population of Puerto Ricans outside Puerto Rico. Eligible islanders received American citizenship in 1917, and after World War II, many came to East Harlem (El Barrio) and the Lower East Side (Loisaida). With them came *mofongo* (page 223), *pernil, tostones*, and other Puerto Rican foods.

Mass immigration from the Dominican Republic to NYC started in the 1960s after the assassination of dictator Rafael Trujillo Molina and the subsequent Dominican Civil War. More Dominicans came in the 1970s and '80s, eventually becoming the second largest Latino population in the city. Most moved to the Washington Heights neighborhood of Manhattan, and the community introduced beach spaghetti (page 59), chimi burgers, *ensalada rusa, mangu*, and other characteristic dishes.

Many Cubans also migrated from the Caribbean to New York City after the Ten Years' War (a rebellion against the Spanish crown), the Spanish-American War, and the Communist Revolution. While not as influential as in Miami, Cuban food and restaurants have captured the city's culinary imagination.

Puebla York
In 1994, after the North American Free Trade Agreement went into effect, a large number of people from Puebla State, Mexico, came to NYC, making Mexicans the third-largest Latino group and forming the city nickname in the header. Poblanos introduced the bodega taquería and, through it, a variety of Pueblan dishes, such as *tacos placeros* and moles (page 78).

LATINO MIDWESTERN
Since the early 1900s, Mexicans and other Latinos have come to the Midwest to work in agriculture, stockyards, meatpacking, manufacturing, construction, and railroads. By 1992, the number of Hispanics in the Midwest reached almost 2 million. Today, more than 2 million Hispanic people live in Illinois alone. Some have called that growth the "browning" of the Midwest. Chicago has the second-largest population of Puerto Ricans outside Puerto Rico as well as the predominantly Mexican neighborhood of Pilsen.

The mothers, sisters, wives, and daughters of migrant workers helped integrate Latino food here by cooking economically, preserving traditions, feeding the community, and sharing their culture with others. These "meat-and-potatoes" comfort foods include Fritados Pie (page 56), Taco Pizza (page 63), Chili Mac (page 109), Mexican Casserole (page 114), Fried Ice Cream (page 144), and more.

Necessity invents variation, and sometimes it calls for shortcuts. Cooking connects us physically with the past, nourishing our souls and our sense of identity, but it also serves the basic purpose of fueling our body. Remember, I'm not a romantic or purist at heart. Fresh tastes best, but if you find yourself pressed for time, money, or energy, it's always fine to buy spices, sauces, and staples rather than making your own, whenever desired or necessary.

Now, let's get cooking.

Breakfast

Desayuno

Café da Manhã

Torrejas de Tres Leches
Rabanadas de Três Leites

The oldest surviving recipe for what we call French toast comes from *On Cooking* by Roman author Apicius, around AD 300. For centuries, people called it "Roman bread" before the English-speaking world christened it "French toast." It eventually became Spanish *torrejas*, served for Semana Santa, and then came to the New World, like so much else, via conquistadores. Some Latin countries and Hispanic communities in America continue the tradition of eating the dish for Holy Week. In Portugal, *rabanadas* originally served as a Christmas dessert, eaten for the *festas de fim de ano* (year-end holidays). Brazilians sometimes dip the bread in syrup or wine, reminiscent of *cantucci* (Tuscan almond biscotti) served with vin santo. In the 1900s, Madrileños also ate them with wine (*torrejas de vino*), and Port or another Portuguese red wine commonly accompanies rabanadas. Today, both America and Latin America have numerous variations of the dish, such as *torrejas salvadoreña, torrejas mexicanas, torrejas cubanas*, and more. Ingredients common to most variations include stale bread (brioche, Mexican *bolillos*, Salvadoran *torta de yema*, and so on), eggs, milk, sugar, cinnamon, and vanilla, but each country tweaks the recipe. Some countries, including Cuba, serve it cold, and Brazil uses a specific bread: *pão de rabanada*. Unlike French toast, torrejas use sweetened milk and sometimes even a sweet spirit, such as rum. A spiced *panela* or *rapadura* syrup—unrefined cane sugar cooked down to something like molasses—typically drizzles over the torrejas, but maple syrup or dulce de leche works just as well.

SERVES 2
Prep Time: 5 MINUTES
Cook Time: 10 MINUTES
Total Time: 15 MINUTES

½ cup whole milk or half-and-half
½ cup sweetened condensed milk
½ cup evaporated milk
1 teaspoon vanilla extract
1 teaspoon ground cinnamon
2 large eggs
Butter for greasing
4 slices day-old or stale bread
   (baguette, bolillo, brioche, challah,
   pan de yema, or similar)
Dulce de Leche (page 228)
Powdered sugar or whipped
   cream (optional)

1. In a medium bowl, whisk together the three milks, vanilla, and cinnamon until well combined.

2. In a small bowl, beat the eggs.

3. Generously butter a medium pan and place it over medium heat.

4. One at a time, gently submerge the bread slices in the milk mixture, then in the beaten eggs.

5. One at a time, fry each slice for 1 to 2 minutes on each side, until golden or golden brown and the centers set.

6. Warm the dulce de leche in a microwave or on the stovetop, then drizzle or spoon it onto the cooked torrejas/rabanadas.

7. Top with powdered sugar or whipped cream, if desired.

TIP

If you prefer denser torrejas/rabanadas, lightly prick both sides of the bread with a fork before dipping (Step 4) so it absorbs more of the mixture.

Molletes

Someone should tell the British about this even more delicious version of beans on toast. Relatively unknown in America before the 1980s, this dish hails from Mexico City. Long before avocado toast rose to popularity, people were eating these open-faced, toasted rolls topped with black beans and cheese for breakfast or an after-school snack. Today, *molletes* appear on the menus of many Texan restaurants and cafés.

SERVES 8
Prep Time: 5 MINUTES
Cook Time: 10 MINUTES
Total Time: 15 MINUTES

4 bolillo rolls

1½ tablespoons unsalted butter, at room temperature

2 cups Refried Beans (page 230) or one 16-ounce can, warmed

1 cup shredded Cheddar or Monterey Jack cheese

½ to 1 cup Pico de Gallo (page 199)

1 avocado (optional)

Hot sauce of choice (optional)

1. Preheat the oven to 350°F.

2. Halve the rolls lengthwise and spread a little more than ½ teaspoon of the butter evenly across each cut side of the bread.

3. Line a baking sheet with foil and place the bread on it, cut side up. Evenly spread ¼ cup of the refried beans onto each buttered roll, followed by 2 tablespoons of the cheese.

4. Bake until the cheese melts, bubbles, and browns, 8 to 10 minutes.

5. Remove from the oven and serve with pico de gallo. Top with avocado and hot sauce, if desired.

VARIATIONS

• You can replace the bolillo rolls with sub bread or a kaiser roll.

• Cheese swaps include provolone, mozzarella, Oaxaca, or Chihuahua.

• Add bacon or Mexican chorizo for a heartier take.

Muhammara Breakfast Sandwiches

A Middle Eastern dip made of roasted red bell peppers, muhammara originated in Aleppo, Syria, which used to have a sizable Jewish community. In the 1940s, many Syrian Jews immigrated to Panama, which many thousands of Sephardim call home today. Panamanians have adopted the dip with gusto. This recipe creates a simple muhammara paste from scratch to slather on a typical American breakfast sandwich.

YIELDS 2 SANDWICHES
Prep Time: 10 MINUTES
Cook Time: 5 MINUTES
Total Time: 15 MINUTES

MUHAMMARA

⅓ cup walnut pieces

3 jarred roasted red bell peppers

½ cup fresh or store-bought
    bread crumbs

2 tablespoons extra-virgin olive oil

1½ tablespoons pomegranate molasses

1 clove garlic

1 teaspoon fresh lemon juice

1 teaspoon Aleppo pepper, or
    ½ teaspoon red pepper flakes

½ teaspoon ground cumin

Salt and freshly ground black pepper

SANDWICH

2 tablespoons unsalted butter

2 brioche or potato buns

4 slices Cheddar cheese

4 strips bacon or 4 slices country ham

2 large eggs

1. Make the muhammara: Preheat the oven to 350°F and line a rimmed baking sheet with aluminum foil.

2. Spread the walnuts evenly on the baking sheet and bake for 4 to 5 minutes. Shake the pan and bake for 4 to 5 more minutes.

3. In a food processor, combine the bell peppers, bread crumbs, roasted walnuts, olive oil, pomegranate molasses, garlic, lemon juice, Aleppo pepper, and cumin and process until they form a creamy mixture. If the muhammara is too thick, add ½ teaspoon of water at a time until it develops a smooth and spreadable consistency. Season with salt and black pepper to taste.

4. Prepare the sandwiches: In a medium skillet over medium heat, heat 1 tablespoon of the butter.

5. Split the buns and place them, cut sides down, in the skillet. Heat until they turn golden brown, 1 or 2 minutes.

6. Immediately remove the buns from the skillet and add 2 slices of cheese to each bottom half, allowing the cheese to warm and melt. Set aside.

7. In the same skillet over medium-high heat, cook the bacon, making sure the pieces don't overlap, until crispy, 4 to 5 minutes. Remove from the pan and drain on a paper towel–lined plate.

8. Add the remaining 1 tablespoon of butter to the skillet, melt, and swirl to coat.

CONTINUES $\longrightarrow$

• Store the muhammara in the refrigerator for up to 5 days.

• To roast your own bell peppers, preheat the oven to 450°F. Line a rimmed baking sheet with aluminum foil. Halve, seed, and trim the bell peppers. Place the peppers, cut side up, on the prepared baking sheet. Brush or drizzle them with olive oil and coat on all sides. Roast until tender and charred in spots, about 20 minutes.

9. Cook the eggs as desired: sunny-side up, over easy, scrambled, etc.

10. Spread 1 tablespoon of muhammara inside the top half of each bun. Add the bacon to bottom bun, then an egg. Assemble the halves and serve warm.

VARIATIONS

• Instead of roasting the walnuts, you can toast them in a skillet over medium heat for 2 to 5 minutes, stirring occasionally with a wooden spoon.

• In lieu of pomegranate molasses, you can use 2 teaspoons of pure maple syrup mixed with 2 teaspoons of fresh lemon juice.

Breakfast Empanadas

I sometimes wonder how my life would look if I were on time more often—probably less stressed but maybe exactly where I am today. From high school, one particularly embarrassing memory lingers. Typically late, I bravely decided not to skip breakfast. Thinking myself ingenious, I scooped scrambled eggs into a plastic storage bag, grabbed a metal fork, and ran to meet my ride. My friends teased me mercilessly. The solution to this predicament wasn't waking earlier and being on time but transforming that morning rush into an empanada. The name derives from *empanar* (to bread), and the dough folds over the filling to make a half-moon shape with a crimped or braided seal called a *repulgue*. Characteristically small, empanadas are meant to be eaten on the go, in a rush. They're food for busy people. (See page 66 for more on the history of empanadas.) This recipe takes inspiration from a traditional American breakfast sandwich, filled with scrambled eggs made with mayo and ham or bacon, all of it fried to golden perfection.

YIELDS 10 EMPANADAS
Prep Time: 5 MINUTES
Cook Time: 15 MINUTES
Total Time: 20 MINUTES

4 large eggs
2 tablespoons mayonnaise
½ cup diced ham or crumbled cooked bacon
½ teaspoon ground coriander
3 tablespoons salted butter
10 Empanada Disks (page 227)
Vegetable or canola oil for frying
¼ cup chopped fresh cilantro
Hot sauce of choice

1. In a medium bowl, whisk together the eggs and mayo. Stir in the ham and coriander.

2. In a medium skillet over medium heat, melt the butter. Scramble the egg mixture slowly until the eggs cook completely, 5 to 7 minutes. Remove from the heat and let cool until cool enough to handle.

3. Place the empanada disks on a flat surface. To each disk, add about 2 tablespoons of the scrambled eggs. Don't overfill.

4. Fold and press the empanada edges together, sealing them with a fork.

5. In a medium skillet over medium-high heat, heat 2 inches of oil. When the surface shimmers or a few flecks of water sizzle on contact, the oil is hot enough.

6. Fry the empanadas, 3 or 4 at a time, until they turn golden and the surface of the dough bubbles, 2 to 3 minutes. Don't overcrowd the pan.

7. Drain the empanadas on a paper towel–lined plate.

8. Transfer to a serving plate, garnish with cilantro, and serve with hot sauce to taste.

Orange Cardamom Masa Harina Pancakes

A traditional type of flour, masa harina makes tamales, tortillas, many other Mexican foods, and now these light and fluffy pancakes. Grinding corn, as is, yields first cornmeal and then finer corn flour. Drying the kernels, cooking them, and steeping them in an alkaline solution, typically food-grade lime (calcium hydroxide)—the whole process called nixtamalization—creates masa harina, which has a savory taste. For the lightest, most aromatic pancakes, use freshly toasted cardamom, if you can. Grind it into a fine powder with a coffee/spice grinder, mortar and pestle, or molcajete (page 201).

YIELDS 12 PANCAKES
Prep Time: 5 MINUTES
Cook Time: 15 MINUTES
Total Time: 20 MINUTES

1 cup masa harina
1 cup all-purpose or gluten-free flour
2 tablespoons granulated sugar
2 teaspoons ground cardamom
½ teaspoon baking powder
½ teaspoon baking soda
½ teaspoon salt
2 large eggs
1½ cups buttermilk, plus more for desired thickness
1 teaspoon orange extract
1 teaspoon vanilla extract (optional)
1 tablespoon orange zest (optional)
2 tablespoons vegetable oil or salted butter, melted
2 tablespoons salted butter for greasing

NOTES

For thicker pancakes, use the given measure of buttermilk. For thinner pancakes, use 2 cups of buttermilk.

1. Preheat the oven to 200°F.

2. In a large bowl, whisk together the flours, sugar, cardamom, baking powder, baking soda, and salt.

3. In a medium bowl, whisk together the eggs, buttermilk, orange extract, vanilla and/or orange zest (if using), and oil.

4. Pour the wet mixture into the dry mixture and mix with a large wooden spoon or rubber spatula until combined. Don't overmix or overbeat. The batter should be thick and fluffy *or* pour easily but not be runny. If you want thinner pancakes but the batter is too thick, add more buttermilk, 1 to 2 tablespoons at a time. If you want tall, fluffy stacks but the batter is too runny, add a little of the two flours in equal parts.

5. Butter a large nonstick skillet and heat it over medium heat.

6. Pour ¼ cup of batter per pancake into the heated pan, spacing them in the skillet so they don't touch. Cook until bubbles form on top and the bottoms turn golden brown, 1 to 2 minutes.

7. With a spatula, flip the pancakes and cook for 1 to 2 more minutes on the other side.

8. Transfer to an oven-safe plate and keep warm in the oven.

CONTINUES $\longrightarrow$

• To make perfect pancake circles, use a baster with measurement markings. If you don't have a baster, transfer thin pancake batter to a small pitcher or large liquid measuring cup. Aim for the middle of the intended pancake circle and pour straight down to the center in one, even stream. Don't move the batter while pouring. A ladle works well, too.

• For thick pancake batter, use an ice cream scoop (between ¼ and ⅓ cup).

9. Repeat with remaining batter, adding more butter to the skillet if necessary.

10. Serve with your favorite toppings: butter, agave syrup, pure maple syrup, powdered sugar, fruit, and so on.

VARIATIONS

• For "pantry" buttermilk, mix 1 tablespoon of white vinegar with 1 cup of milk, stir, and let rest for 5 minutes before using. You also can replace the vinegar with fresh lemon juice or 1½ teaspoons cream of tartar.

• In lieu of cardamom, try cinnamon.

• The citrus flavor of orange extract will permeate every pancake, but you can replace that with ½ teaspoon of orange liqueur (such as Cointreau or Grand Marnier) or the juice of ½ orange.

Breakfast Tacos

A delicious marriage of Mexican and German ingredients, Breakfast Tacos require flour tortillas and eggs, and typically contain potatoes, cheese, and a protein of choice, such as chorizo, bacon, beans, or tofu. Some food historians argue that the dish hails from the Rio Grande Valley of New Mexico or migrated as is from northern Mexico, but these morning tacos most likely originated in the kitchens of immigrant Mexican families living in Texas, the birthplace of so many American Latino foods, most notably Tex-Mex. Within the Lone Star State, controversy still surrounds the dish's birthplace. Austin, the capital, has become the country's go-to destination for morning tacos, but the earliest reference to them, in the *Arizona Republic* in 1975, records them as being served in San Antonio. The battle for bragging rights grew so heated that the mayors of Austin and San Antonio came together in 2016 to call a truce. See page 52 for more on the history of the taco.

SERVES 4
Prep Time: 10 MINUTES
Cook Time: 15 MINUTES
Total Time: 25 MINUTES

1 large russet potato
1 teaspoon salt
1 tablespoon vegetable oil
¼ small yellow onion
4 ounces ground spicy chorizo
3 large eggs
Salt and freshly ground black pepper
2 tablespoons unsalted butter
4 Flour Tortillas (page 215)
½ cup grated Cheddar cheese
Sour cream, avocado, hot sauce, and/or
    fresh cilantro for serving

1. Peel the potato and dice it into ½-inch pieces.

2. In a large pot, place the potato pieces, cover with cold water, and add salt. Bring to a boil, then lower the heat to low and simmer until the potato pieces become tender and a fork easily pierces them, 3 to 5 minutes. Drain, pat dry with a paper towel, and set aside.

3. In a large skillet over medium heat, heat the oil.

4. Meanwhile, dice the onion.

5. Add the onion and ground chorizo to the skillet. Cook, stirring occasionally, until the chorizo starts to brown and the onion softens, 5 to 7 minutes.

6. Spread the drained potato pieces evenly in the skillet. Cook for 2 to 3 minutes, flip them, and cook for 2 to 3 more minutes, until they begin to brown and crisp, the chorizo has cooked through, and the onion has become translucent. Remove from the heat and set aside.

7. In a medium bowl, whisk together the eggs, salt, and pepper for about 30 seconds.

8. With a paper towel, wipe the skillet, add the butter, melt it over medium-low heat, and swirl to coat evenly.

CONTINUES $\longrightarrow$

• If your homemade tortillas are a few days old and not as pliable, brush them with a little water before warming.

• Keep the tortillas warm in a *tortillero* or by covering them with a clean, slightly dampened dish towel. For oven-warmed tortillas, preheat the oven to 350°F. Wrap a stack of no more than 5 tortillas with aluminum foil. Heat in the oven for 15 to 20 minutes, until heated through.

VARIATIONS

• For the chorizo, you can substitute bacon, *carne guisada*, vegan "meat" of choice, beans, or tofu.

• For spicy sour cream, add hot sauce to taste and whisk together.

9. Add the eggs to the skillet and cook for 30 seconds to 1 minute without disturbing.

10. Between 1 and 2 minutes, when the eggs are about three-quarters of the way done, use a rubber spatula or wooden spoon to fold the eggs and form big, fluffy curds.

11. Turn off the heat but keep the eggs in the skillet until just set and still moist.

12. While the eggs set, warm the tortillas in a large, dry skillet over medium heat for about 30 seconds each. Alternatively, use heatproof tongs to warm the tortillas directly over a flame for a few seconds. When warm, plate them.

13. Divide the cheese equally among the tortillas. Top each with a scoop of the potato-chorizo mixture and a scoop of the eggs.

14. Serve with sour cream, sliced avocado, hot sauce, and/or cilantro.

San Antonio Migas

The Payaya people first settled what has become the San Antonio area, calling it Yanaguana, meaning "refreshing waters." In 1691, the Spanish arrived on the feast day of St. Anthony of Padua, renaming it in his honor. In 1716, the viceroy of New Spain authorized the creation of San Fernando de Béxar, a Spanish settlement, to block French expansion from Louisiana. It eventually became the capital of the Tejas province. *Migas* means "crumbs" in Spanish, and the dish's lineage reaches back to Spain and Portugal. European versions use day-old bread, whereas the Mexican version, a dish born of war, uses corn tortillas. During the Mexican Revolution (1910–1920), food grew scarce, and people had to eat every crumb they had. At heart, Mexican migas consist of fried strips of day-old tortillas served with scrambled eggs. But migas served in Mexico City today look very different. In *migas tepitanas* (Tepita-style migas), sliced day-old bolillos, a type of bread, thicken hot garlic soup. The heat of the soup slowly cooks a raw egg dropped into it. Some of the earliest references to migas in Texas appear in *La Prensa de San Antonio* in 1922 and the *Brownsville Herald* in 1951. A Tex-Mex scramble, San Antonio migas make an affordable and satisfying meal, after a night out, to soak up alcohol—which is how I first had it when living in Alamo City—or, in this case, for breakfast. It features short strips of fried corn tortilla, onion, bell pepper, and chili powder, served with cheese and pico de gallo and/or salsa. As with most American adaptations, the Tex-Mex version has a lot more toppings. It's not a beautiful dish (page 25), but it's easy to make (even after a few drinks) and hits the spot.

SERVES 2

Prep Time: 10 MINUTES

Cook Time: 15 MINUTES

Total Time: 25 MINUTES

3 large eggs

1 teaspoon salt

½ teaspoon toasted ground cumin

3 tablespoons vegetable oil

Three 4- to 6-inch Corn Tortillas
(page 210)

1 Jalapeño pepper

1 clove garlic

¼ cup diced white onion

¼ cup diced red or green bell pepper

1 cup freshly grated mozzarella,
Monterey Jack, or Mexican
blend cheese

1 medium avocado, pitted, peeled, and
sliced (optional)

¼ cup Pico de Gallo (page 199)

¼ cup Salsa Roja (page 217)

¼ cup chopped fresh cilantro

1. Position a rack in the center of the oven and preheat it to 350°F.

2. In a medium bowl, whisk together the eggs, salt, and cumin and set aside.

3. In a medium nonstick, ovenproof skillet over medium heat, heat the oil.

4. Meanwhile, cut the tortillas into ¼-inch strips.

5. Fry the tortilla strips, stirring occasionally, until crisp, about 2 minutes.

6. While the tortilla strips fry, seed and finely chop the Jalapeño pepper and mince the garlic.

7. Add the onion, bell peppers, and Jalapeño pepper to the tortilla strips. Cook, stirring frequently, until the vegetables soften, about 5 minutes.

8. Add the garlic and cook until fragrant, 1 more minute.

9. Add the eggs and stir to combine all the ingredients. Continue to cook, stirring often, until the eggs just set.

10. Top evenly with the cheese, transfer the skillet to the oven, and bake until the cheese melts, about 8 minutes.

11. Divide the cooked eggs between two plates and top with sliced avocado (if using), pico de gallo, salsa roja, and cilantro.

How to Scramble Eggs Perfectly

Prep your pan first so the eggs will start cooking as soon as they hit it: Setting the heat to medium-low for a few minutes allows the heat to distribute evenly first throughout the pan and then throughout the eggs.

To the preheated pan, add 1 pat of butter or 1 teaspoon of oil per egg.

In a bowl, whisk the eggs, season to preference, and pour them into the pan. If they sizzle, the pan is too hot. In that case, turn down the heat.

For big, fluffy curds, let the eggs sit undisturbed for 1 to 2 minutes. When the edges of the eggs have set, lightly use a spatula to move, pull, and fold the eggs around the pan. Let them set a bit more and repeat. Excessive stirring results in smaller curds and a crumbly scramble. If bits of egg stick to the sides or bottom of the pan when you stir, gently use the spatula to lift them so they don't burn.

When your eggs are about three-quarters of the way cooked, remove the pan from the heat. Residual heat will finish cooking the eggs while maintaining moisture, so they stay creamy instead of drying out. When done, they should look slightly firm, have no runny or undercooked yolks, and glisten with a solid yellow color.

New Mexico Breakfast Burritos

Ancient Pueblo peoples lived extensively throughout what today is New Mexico, and Aztec knowledge of their societies created the myth of the Seven Cities of Gold that lured the Spanish through North America. As a province of New Spain, New Mexico joined the rest of Mexico after the Mexican War of Independence ended in 1821. When Texas seceded from Mexico in 1836, it claimed roughly half of modern New Mexico, and, after the Mexican-American War, the Treaty of Guadalupe Hidalgo transferred the other half to the United States in 1848. It remained a federal territory until 1912, when it joined the Union. The breakfast burrito entered New Mexican cuisine in the 1970s, when the Albuquerque International Balloon Fiesta served a handheld version and then Tia Sophia's, a restaurant in Santa Fe, smothered it with cheese and sauce. New Mexico breakfast burritos require flour tortillas, shredded hash browns, eggs, and of course New Mexico chiles. Using both red and green chiles and sauce aptly creates "Christmas" burritos. New Mexico chiles, or Hatch chiles if they grow in the Hatch Valley, have a reputation for their flavor and versatility. New Mexico State University cultivated the green chile pepper, but red and green varieties come from the same plant, just picked at different times. The green chiles taste buttery yet smoky, while the red ones taste sweeter.

SERVES 4

Prep Time: 5 MINUTES
Cook Time: 25 MINUTES
Total Time: 30 MINUTES

Four 10-inch Flour Tortillas (page 215)
1 medium yellow onion
5 tablespoons vegetable or olive oil
1 pound frozen shredded hash browns
Salt and freshly ground black pepper
6 slices bacon
1 cup grated Cheddar or Monterey Jack cheese
6 large eggs
2 tablespoons unsalted butter
One 4-ounce can or jar diced green chiles
2 ounces canned or jarred diced red chiles
Salsa Roja (page 217) and Salsa Verde (page 226), or red and green enchilada sauces

1. Preheat the oven to 400°F.

2. Arrange the tortillas on a baking sheet and set aside.

3. Chop the onion.

4. In a large nonstick skillet over medium-high heat, heat 2 tablespoons of the oil. Add the onion, lower the heat to medium-low, and cook until translucent, 5 to 7 minutes.

5. Add the frozen hash browns, season with salt and black pepper to taste, and increase the heat to medium-high. Cook until the hash browns turn brown and crispy, 3 to 5 minutes on each side, adding more oil, 1 teaspoon at a time, if necessary. Transfer the hash brown mixture to a paper towel–lined plate.

6. Wipe the skillet with a paper towel, add 1 teaspoon of the oil, and cook the bacon strips until crispy, 3 to 4 minutes. Transfer to a second paper towel–lined plate. Leave the strips whole or crumble if desired.

CONTINUES →

• If you can find them, use ½ cup of roasted, chopped New Mexico green chiles instead of canned.

• Refrigerate the burritos for up to 24 hours and reheat in a microwave or oven.

7. Divide the hash brown mixture and bacon equally among the tortillas. Top each with ¼ cup of the cheese. Place the baking sheet in the oven while you prepare the eggs.

8. Place the eggs in a large bowl and whisk for 30 seconds. Add salt and black pepper to taste.

9. With a paper towel, wipe the skillet again and place it over medium-low heat. Add the butter and, as it melts, swirl to coat.

10. Cook the whisked eggs in the skillet for 30 seconds to 1 minute without disturbing.

11. Between 1 and 2 minutes, when the eggs are about three-quarters of the way done, use a rubber spatula or wooden spoon to fold the eggs and form big, fluffy curds.

12. Turn off heat but keep the eggs in the skillet until just set and still moist.

13. Quarter the eggs and place each serving next to the hash browns on the tortillas.

14. To each tortilla, add 2 tablespoons of green chiles and 1 tablespoon of red chiles.

15. Fold the left and right sides of each tortilla over the filling, then roll tightly, from the bottom up, over the filling.

16. Repeat with the remaining burritos. Top with the two sauces to taste.

Pineapple Granola

I used to sell granola wholesale to boutique hotels in the Nolita neighborhood of Manhattan. In my small apartment kitchen, I baked 25 to 50 pounds of it every week and carted it in a food-grade bin. I couldn't afford taxis and feared it might fall down the subway stairs and scatter everywhere, so I walked it downtown myself. A friend who worked as a restaurateur and hotelier became my first customer. His mother had died, so with my condolences, I gave him a jar. He popped open the lid, threw a handful in his mouth, and said, "Ah, this is the caviar of granola!" (He's French.) I didn't wind up going into the granola business, so now, on rare occasions, I bake it only for family or a special someone. This *granola de piña* adapts the original with rich, tropical flavors. The original recipe will remain a secret.

SERVES 5
Prep Time: 5 MINUTES
Cook Time: 25 MINUTES
Total Time: 30 MINUTES

2 cups old-fashioned rolled oats
⅓ cup raw cashew pieces
¼ teaspoon kosher salt
2 tablespoons coconut sugar
   or raw sugar
¼ cup extra-virgin coconut oil
⅓ cup pure maple syrup or honey
1 teaspoon vanilla extract
¼ cup dried pineapple chunks
¼ cup coconut flakes

1. Preheat the oven to 350°F and line a baking sheet with parchment paper.

2. In a medium bowl, combine the oats, cashews, salt, and coconut sugar.

3. In a small microwave-safe bowl, microwave the coconut oil on low in 30-second increments until it melts.

4. Whisk in the maple syrup and vanilla until combined.

5. Add the oil mixture to the oat mixture and stir to coat and moisten the oats evenly.

6. With a spatula, spread the raw granola evenly on the baking sheet and bake for 15 minutes.

7. Stir the granola, rotate the pan, and bake for 5 to 10 more minutes, until the granola smells fragrant and turns a light golden color. Don't let the nuts burn.

8. Remove from the oven and let cool to room temperature. The granola may appear a little oily or wet, but it will dry as it cools.

9. Transfer to a large bowl and combine with the pineapple chunks and coconut flakes.

10. Serve on its own, with yogurt and a drizzle of agave syrup as pictured, or with milk of choice as a hearty cereal.

Tex-Mex Green Chilaquiles con Sombrero

The word *chilaquiles* comes from the Nahuatl language of central Mexico, and the dish helpfully repurposes stale tortillas, the main ingredient. It comes in two sauce variations: green, as in this recipe, and red. The "sombrero" refers to the fried egg that tops the dish. The first printed reference to chilaquiles appears in *El Cocinero Español* by Encarnación Pinedo, the first Mexican-American cookbook, published in San Francisco in 1898. It first appears in Texas in a 1925 issue of *La Prensa de San Antonio*. Everything really is bigger in Texas, including this Tex-Mex breakfast favorite. People often confuse migas (page 16), pictured at bottom right, with chilaquiles, on the top right, but migas contain tortilla strips and require scrambled eggs, whereas chilaquiles use triangular tortilla chips with eggs optional.

SERVES 4

Prep Time: 10 MINUTES
Cook Time: 20 MINUTES
Total Time: 30 MINUTES

1 tablespoon vegetable oil
½ cup chopped red onion
¼ cup water
1½ cups Salsa Verde (page 226)
½ cup corn kernels, fresh, drained from a can, or frozen
12 Corn Tortilla Chips (page 206), their oiled skillet set aside and reserved
4 large eggs
⅓ cup green onions
1 cup shredded Monterey Jack cheese
⅓ cup chopped fresh cilantro
1 tablespoon fresh lime juice
Pico de Gallo (page 199) and avocado for garnish (optional)

1. In a large lidded skillet over medium-high heat, heat the vegetable oil and cook the red onion until it softens and starts to turn translucent, 3 to 4 minutes.

2. Add the water to the skillet and stir to loosen any brown bits.

3. Lower the heat to medium, add the salsa verde, and cook for 5 minutes, stirring frequently.

4. Add the corn and tortilla chips to the salsa verde and stir to combine.

5. In the skillet used to fry the tortilla chips, fry the eggs sunny-side up or over easy.

6. While the eggs fry, thinly slice the green onions.

7. Top the sauced tortilla chips with the cheese, cilantro, and green onions. Cover, lower the heat to low, and simmer just until the cheese melts, about 2 minutes.

8. Sprinkle with lime juice, top with the fried eggs, and garnish with pico de gallo and chopped avocado (if using).

VARIATIONS

• You can use store-bought, but the Salsa Verde on page 226 goes specifically with these chilaquiles.

• To make this recipe with epazote: After Step 2, add 2 more teaspoons of vegetable oil to the skillet over medium heat, add 2 or 3 epazote sprigs with the red onions, and fry for 3 to 5 minutes. Then, for Step 3, add the salsa verde and cook until the epazote wilts, 30 seconds to 1 minute. Remove the epazote before adding the corn and tortillas.

• For chilaquiles rojos, use the Salsa Roja recipe on page 217.

Huevos Divorciados Shakshuka

Shakshuka, eggs poached in a tomato sauce, hails from northwest Africa. Sometime in the mid-1500s, after Hernán Cortés de Monroy y Pizarro Altamirano toppled the Aztec Empire, he introduced tomatoes to the region. In the 1950s and '60s, North African Jews brought the dish to Israel, and from there it spread to other Jewish enclaves around the world, including New York City. I first tried it at Café Mogador in the East Village, which called it Moroccan eggs. *Huevos divorciados* (divorced eggs), a traditional Mexican breakfast, consists of fried eggs served partly on salsa verde and partly on salsa roja, separate but sharing the same dish, all of it over tortillas. Born of colonization and diaspora, this recipe grafts the two into a tasty union of Old World and New.

SERVES 4 TO 6
Prep Time: 5 MINUTES
Cook Time: 45 MINUTES
Total Time: 50 MINUTES

TOMATO SAUCE

2 pounds ripe plum tomatoes, or one 28-ounce can tomatoes
3 tablespoons vegetable oil
1 small yellow onion
6 to 8 dried árbol chiles
1 clove garlic
¼ teaspoon ground cinnamon
Salt

SHAKSHUKA

Cooking spray
2 cups Refried Beans (page 230), warmed
12 ounces Salsa Verde (page 226)
6 large eggs
Salt and freshly ground black pepper
¼ cup grated Cotija cheese
¼ cup crema Mexicana
Fresh cilantro for garnish
Corn Tortillas (page 210) or Flour Tortillas (page 215) for serving

NOTE

The tomato sauce in this recipe may look similar to Salsa Roja (page 217), but it includes important differences, so don't substitute the latter here.

1. If using fresh tomatoes, stem them. Place the tomatoes in a large pot, add enough water to cover them, and bring to a boil over high heat. Lower the heat to low and simmer until they soften, about 15 minutes. Drain, then blend them in a blender until smooth. Skip boiling if using canned tomatoes. Meanwhile, slice the onion.

2. In a medium skillet over medium-low heat, combine the oil, onion, chiles, garlic, and cinnamon. Cook, stirring, until the onion softens and the garlic becomes fragrant, 4 to 7 minutes.

3. Add the tomato puree or canned tomatoes and simmer, stirring frequently, until the mixture thickens, about 15 minutes. Add salt to taste and pulse in a blender until mostly smooth but still thick with texture. Set aside.

4. Meanwhile, prepare the shakshuka: Preheat the oven to 375°F and lightly coat a medium oven-safe skillet with cooking spray.

5. Spread the refried beans evenly in the skillet, creating a slight wall all along the middle. Gently pour the salsa verde on one side of the wall and the tomato sauce on the other.

6. Crack 3 of the eggs into the tomato sauce and the other 3 into the salsa verde. Season the eggs with salt and black pepper to taste.

7. Put the skillet into the oven and bake until the eggs just set, 7 to 10 minutes.

8. Remove the skillet from the oven. Sprinkle the shakshuka with the Cotija cheese, dollop with the crema Mexicana, and garnish with cilantro. Serve with warm corn or flour tortillas.

Guava Cream Cheese Cinnamon Rolls

In northern Virginia, the first time I set foot in an American mall, the overpowering scent of sugar and cinnamon hit me. After cruising past the vanilla and cucumber smells of Bath & Body Works, I came upon the last spot on the gameboard of the Candy Land mall: Cinnabon. Topped with cream cheese frosting, those fluffy sugar and cinnamon swirls ignited my never-ending love affair with cinnamon buns. From that point forward, every new city that I visited required a search for the best cinnamon bun. (Ann Sather in Chicago holds my heart for the best.) Even the orange-glazed cinnamon rolls that come in a tube delighted me, a special weekend treat for my sister and me after we completed our weekend chores. Guava perfectly pairs with cinnamon and cream cheese. This recipe layers guava paste with cinnamon inside the rolls and incorporates the hearty tropical fruit into the cream cheese frosting, giving this treat a light pink hue. See page 133 for more about the origins of the delicious union of guava and cream cheese.

YIELDS 12
Prep Time: 45 MINUTES
Cook Time: 1 HOUR 15 MINUTES
Total Time: 2 HOURS

DOUGH

1 cup whole milk

½ cup granulated sugar

1 tablespoon active dry yeast

6 tablespoons salted butter, melted

2 large eggs, at room temperature

1 teaspoon vanilla extract

4 cups all-purpose flour, plus ½ cup for consistency if necessary, and more for dusting

1 teaspoon salt

1 teaspoon ground cinnamon

Unsalted butter, at room temperature, for greasing

Cooking spray

FILLING

8 ounces guava paste, cubed

⅔ cup packed light brown sugar

2 tablespoons ground cinnamon

6 tablespoons salted butter, at room temperature

FROSTING

8 ounces cream cheese, at room temperature

4 ounces guava paste, cubed

¼ cup salted butter, at room temperature

2 cups powdered sugar

½ teaspoon vanilla extract

⅛ teaspoon salt

CONTINUES $\longrightarrow$

1. Make the dough: In a large, microwave-safe bowl of a stand mixer, microwave the milk at full power for 45 to 60 seconds.

2. Add 1 tablespoon of the granulated sugar and the yeast, stir, and let sit until it becomes foamy, about 5 minutes.

3. Add the remaining granulated sugar, butter, eggs, and vanilla; stir to combine; then add the 4 cups of flour, salt, and cinnamon.

4. Fit the stand mixer with a dough hook, place the bowl on the stand, and set the speed to low. Gradually increase the speed to high until a large ball forms.

5. Remove the dough ball and knead until smooth and slightly tacky to the touch. If the dough is too sticky and doesn't form a ball, add more flour, 1 tablespoon at a time, but no more than ½ cup.

6. On a lightly floured surface, knead the dough for 3 to 5 minutes, until smooth.

7. Butter a large bowl with the room-temperature butter.

8. Shape the dough into a ball, place it into the buttered bowl, and cover the bowl loosely with plastic wrap or a clean, damp towel.

9. In a warm place, let the dough rise until it doubles in size, 30 to 45 minutes. Don't let it overrise.

10. While the dough rises, make the filling: In a mixing bowl, use a hand mixer to beat the guava paste until light and fluffy, starting slowly and gradually increasing the speed.

11. Scrape down the sides of the bowl, add the remaining filling ingredients, and beat until incorporated. Set aside.

12. Next, assemble and bake the rolls: Preheat the oven to 350°F, lightly spray a 9-by-13-inch glass baking dish with cooking spray, and lightly dust a large, flat, clean surface with flour.

13. Gently punch down the risen dough and, on the floured surface, form it into a rectangle.

14. With a rolling pin, roll the dough into a 12-by-24-inch rectangle, about ¼ inch thick. Note: The exact size of the rectangle can vary.

15. Spray a silicone or offset spatula with cooking spray and use it to spread the filling evenly over the dough.

16. Starting on the long end, tightly roll the dough into a log.

17. Cut the log into 12 equal-sized rolls, each about 2 inches wide.

18. Place the rolls horizontally in the glass baking dish in a 3-by-4 grid.

19. Cover the dish loosely with plastic wrap and let the rolls rise until they nearly double in size, 20 to 30 minutes.

20. Remove the plastic wrap and bake until golden brown, 20 to 25 minutes. If the tops brown too rapidly, tent the baking dish with foil and continue to bake. When done, the internal temperature of the rolls, taken with an instant-read thermometer, should measure between 195° and 200°F.

21. Remove the baking dish from the oven, place on a cooling rack, and let the rolls cool for 5 to 10 minutes.

22. While the rolls cool, make the frosting: In the bowl of a stand mixer fitted with a paddle attachment, beat the cream cheese on high speed until smooth, about 2 minutes.

23. Add the guava paste and butter and mix until smoothly combined. Gradually add the powdered sugar, vanilla, and salt until incorporated as well.

24. With a knife or icing spatula, spread the icing over the warm rolls and serve immediately.

NOTE

"Warm" means between 105° and 115°F.

Pan Cubano

Cuban bread forms an integral part of Floribbean cuisine, but an Italo-Spanish immigrant invented it. Born in Sicily, Francisco Ferlita founded La Joven Francesca bakery in the Ybor City neighborhood of Tampa, Florida, in 1896. The bakery became famous for its Cuban bread, and since then, the dish has become a South Florida staple. But I had a memorable encounter with bread made on the island, *pan alimento*, while at a homestay in Havana. In the 1950s, the Communist Revolution dispersed my Cuban family—which is why I was born in Panama—so we all gathered on the island nation for a reunion. One late, hot night, I snuck away from my *casa particular*. I was feeling restless and wandered to cool off and tire myself out. The scent of baking bread hung thick in the air. It led me to the only fluorescent-lit building in the street: a bread factory. Inside, a conveyor belt whirred while men labored to prepare bread for the next day's ration booklet, *la libreta de abastecimiento*. They made and ate it to survive, which, in that moment, made me feel ashamed of my privilege. Then that moment of clarity evolved. Home bakers can and should indulge in the art of making Cuban bread as much as any other kind. With a soft, almost papery crust and a light chew, Pan Cubano literally serves as the foundation for Cuban Sandwiches (page 82), but it also works wonderfully as a light breakfast, slightly toasted, with a lick of jam or guava paste, served with *café con leche*.

YIELDS 2 LOAVES
Prep Time: 13 HOURS
Cook Time: 30 MINUTES
Total Time: 13 HOURS 30 MINUTES

STARTER

⅜ teaspoon active dry yeast

2 tablespoons plus 2 teaspoons all-purpose flour

Scant 2 tablespoons warm water (about 100°F)

DOUGH

4½ teaspoons active dry yeast

1 tablespoon granulated sugar

1½ cups warm water (about 100°F)

6 tablespoons lard or vegetable shortening

1 tablespoon salt

6 cups all-purpose flour, plus more for dusting

2 teaspoons vegetable oil

Cornmeal or semolina for dusting

1. Make the starter: In a small bowl or measuring cup, whisk together the yeast, flour, and warm water until well blended. Cover with plastic wrap and refrigerate overnight or at least 8 hours.

2. When the yeast starter has chilled, make the dough: In a large bowl, combine the dry yeast, sugar, and warm water. Let the mixture rest for 15 minutes. The yeast should be bubbling on the surface.

3. Add the lard, salt, and 2 cups of the flour. Mix until incorporated and the dough forms a sticky ball.

4. Add the starter and 3½ cups of the remaining flour. Mix to incorporate.

5. On a lightly floured surface, knead the dough until it forms a firm ball. Add the remaining flour as needed. The dough should feel soft and supple yet slightly tacky. It should stick but then release from your hands, leaving no mess.

6. In a large bowl, place the dough and coat its surface completely with the oil.

CONTINUES →

NOTES

• In South Florida, a palmetto frond placed atop the unbaked loaf creates the bread's seam, a practice dating back to La Joven Francesca Bakery. As the bread bakes, the frond gently rises. The area under the leaves remains moist and soft, and the seam allows hot gases to escape. If you don't have palmetto fronds, you can create the seams in other ways.

• While the raw loaf proofs, prepare your scoring device. For a palmetto frond, cut 2 long strips. Rinse in hot water, then dry. Put the fronds or skewers diagonally along the prepared baking sheets and place the shaped dough on top. Proof per the directions. Before baking, gently flip the bread over so the fronds or skewers are on top. For baker's twine, dampen thick pieces, about 18 inches long, in warm water. Lay them along the top length of each loaf. Press down just a little, then proof and bake as directed.

• In the oven, the *baño maria* (bain-marie) creates the water vapor necessary to make Cuban bread. If you don't have a metal casserole dish, fill a clean spray bottle with water and lightly mist the raw loaves prior to placing them in the oven, as pictured.

7. Cover the bowl with a damp kitchen towel and place in a warm spot to rise. Let it at least double in size, about 2 hours.

8. Line 2 baking sheets with parchment paper, sprinkle the paper with cornmeal, and set aside.

9. Transfer the dough to a lightly floured surface and flour your hands.

10. Halve the dough and shape each half into a 4- to 5-inch-by-12-inch rectangle that's ½ inch thick.

11. Starting at the long sides, tightly roll the rectangles to form 2 skinny loaves.

12. Pinch the seams and ends to seal and slightly flatten the tops.

13. Transfer the raw loaves to the prepared baking sheets and dust them with flour.

14. With palmetto fronds, skewers, baker's twine, a lame, or a sharp knife (as pictured), score the loaves.

15. Cover each loaf with a clean, light, dry towel or lightly with plastic wrap and let rise until doubled in size, 1½ to 2 hours.

16. Place a metal casserole dish on the lowest rack of the oven and preheat it to 400°F.

17. Place the baking sheets on the middle rack, pour 1 to 2 cups of water into the preheated casserole dish, and quickly shut the oven door.

18. Bake until the bread turns golden brown, about 25 minutes, removing the casserole dish of water during the last 5 minutes of baking.

19. Remove from the oven, transfer loaves to a cooling rack, and let cool to room temperature before slicing.

TIP

If you double the starter ingredients to ¾ teaspoon of active dry yeast, ⅓ cup of all-purpose flour, and ⅓ cup of warm water, you can save half in an airtight container in the fridge for the next time you bake bread.

Lunch

Almuerzo

Almoço

Mango Chile Salad

Years ago, one of my best friends shared a version of this salad with me, which I've tweaked over the years. We ate it in her closet-size apartment in the West Village above the Porto Rico coffee shop. Chamoy originates with dried, salted plums or berries that, after Spanish colonization of the Philippines, Chinese immigrants brought to the archipelago. In Cantonese, *chàhn pèih múi* is salted plum peel, which became *champoy* in Filipino, meaning pickled dried fruits. In Mexico, chamoy now specifies just the sauce—made from dehydrated apricots, mangoes, plums, or a combination; chili powder; salt; sugar; and citrus juice—while the pickled fruits themselves are called *saladitos* ("little salty things"). Vendors around New York City sell chile-dusted, chamoy-covered mangoes on a stick, a simple but unexpectedly nuanced treat. Like the sauce and powdered condiment that inspired it, this salad tastes salty, sour, spicy, and sweet.

SERVES 2
Prep Time: 10 MINUTES
Total Time: 10 MINUTES

SALAD
1 bunch lacinato (dinosaur) kale
1 Ataúlfo mango
1 large lemon or lime
1 to 2 tablespoons extra-virgin olive oil
Kosher salt
2 tablespoons finely chopped red onion

DRESSING
2 tablespoons olive oil
2 teaspoons honey
Freshly ground black pepper and salt
Crushed red pepper flakes or
    chili powder

NOTE

For homemade Tajín, combine 1 tablespoon paprika or red chili powder, 1 teaspoon dried lime zest, ½ teaspoon ground cumin, ¼ teaspoon garlic powder, ¼ teaspoon ground cayenne pepper, ¼ teaspoon ground coriander, ¼ teaspoon onion powder, ¼ teaspoon sea salt, and ⅛ teaspoon granulated sugar.

1. Make the salad: Wash and dry the kale. Separate the leaves from the ribs. Discard the ribs and chop the leaves into ribbons.

2. Peel and pit the mango and chop it into small chunks.

3. Juice the lemon or lime.

4. In a large bowl, combine the kale, olive oil, half of the citrus juice (about 1 tablespoon), and kosher salt to taste. Gently massage the kale ribbons until soft, about 1 minute.

5. Add the mango and red onion and set aside.

6. Make the dressing: In a small bowl, whisk together the remaining citrus juice, olive oil, honey, a few grinds of black pepper and shakes of salt, and red pepper flakes to taste.

7. Dress the salad and toss to coat.

VARIATIONS

• You can use green kale for this recipe, but it will require 1 to 2 more minutes of massaging to soften the leaves.

• If you can't find Ataúlfo mangoes, use your mango of choice.

• To celebrate this salad's roots, drizzle it with chamoy sauce instead of or in addition to the dressing.

Puerto Rican Party Sandwiches

"It's not a party without a *sandwich de mezcla*!" said Marta Rivera Diaz, a recipe developer, chef, and friend. When we first met in San Antonio, she told me about these party sandwiches, which remind me of the pimiento cheese sandwiches popular in much of the American South. This thrifty nibble consists of white bread, jarred cheese, and canned ham—nothing fancy but a requisite for Boricua food gatherings. Some people prefer a creamier, almost liquid consistency for these *sandwichitos*, in which case omit the cream cheese. Trimming the crusts is traditional.

YIELDS 40 SANDWICH TRIANGLES
Prep Time: 10 MINUTES
Total Time: 10 MINUTES

12 ounces lunch meat, such as Jamonilla or SPAM brand

1 cup Queso Blanco (page 208) or jarred cheese dip, such as Cheez Whiz or Velveeta brand, at room temperature

4 ounces cream cheese, at room temperature (optional)

4 ounces canned diced pimientos or jarred red bell peppers, including juice

40 slices white bread (2 loaves)

Grape or cherry tomatoes for garnish (optional)

1. Cube the lunch meat.

2. In a food processor, process the queso blanco, cream cheese (if using), pimientos, and lunch meat until well combined and smooth.

3. On 1 slice of bread, spread 2 tablespoons of the processed mixture. Top with another slice of bread, trim the crusts, and halve into triangles.

4. Repeat with the remaining spread and bread.

5. Garnish with halved grape or cherry tomatoes, if desired.

The Original Nachos

Few Latino dishes have become as ubiquitous as nachos, but this is the source from which all other nacho recipes spring. In 1940, in the Victory Club of Piedras Negras, Mexico—across the Rio Grande from Eagle Pass, Texas—a regular named Mamie Finan asked Ignacio "Nacho" Anaya, the maître d'hôtel, to make her and her friends a new snack. In a moment of hospitality genius, he threw together corn tortilla chips, Colby cheese, and slices of pickled Jalapeño peppers. When the ladies who lunch asked what it was, he called it "Nacho's Special." The word "nachos" first appears in English in 1949 in *A Taste of Texas*, a cookbook compiled by Jane Trahey for the Neiman Marcus department store, which began in Dallas. Endless variations of the instant hit have followed—even for religious holidays. Instead of corn tortillas, "machos" use matzo for Passover.

SERVES 6 TO 8
Prep Time: 5 MINUTES
Cook Time: 7 MINUTES
Total Time: 12 MINUTES

16 ounces Corn Tortilla Chips
   (page 206)
2 cups grated Colby cheese
2 cups grated Cheddar cheese
1 cup thinly sliced pickled
   Jalapeño peppers
2 to 4 tablespoons pickled Jalapeño
   pepper brine

1. Place racks in the lower and upper thirds of the oven and preheat it to 400°F.

2. On 2 large, unlined baking sheets, spread the tortilla chips in single layers.

3. In a large bowl, mix the cheeses together.

4. Over each tortilla chip, sprinkle 1 tablespoon of the combined cheeses and top each with 1 or 2 slices of pickled Jalapeño pepper.

5. Sprinkle or spoon the Jalapeño brine over all the chips.

6. Bake until the cheese melts, 5 to 7 minutes.

7. Serve immediately, either on the baking sheets or using a hard spatula to transfer them to a serving platter.

Misto-Quente Sliders

Hawaii has a long, fruitful relationship with Latino cultures. Around 1793, Francisco de Paula Marín arrived in Hawaii, where he became an adviser to King Kamehameha I, who planted many European fruits and vegetables that the Spanish brought, including the first pineapple in 1813. King Kamehameha III invited vaqueros from Spanish California to teach his people how to handle cattle. After a hurricane devastated Puerto Rico's sugar plantations in 1900, the Hawaiian Sugar Planters' Association recruited thousands of Puerto Ricans to the Pacific, where they now form the largest part of Hawaii's growing Latino demographic. Notable Hawaiian dishes that came from Puerto Rico include *ensalada de bacalao*, gandule rice, *pasteles*, and the Lava Flow, a version of the Piña Colada (page 182). Portuguese immigrants from the Azores and Madeira brought *pão doce* (sweet bread) with them, and it was given the New World name of Hawaiian rolls. In 2015, diplomatic relations between America and Cuba resumed, and the Cubanakoa Foundation has worked to establish a sister-city relationship between Honolulu and Havana. If you've never eaten Portuguese sweet bread or Hawaiian rolls, they taste like a fluffy, sweeter potato roll, combining beautifully with savory meat and the sharp tang of condiments. These small rolls make it easier to feed a crowd with single-serving portions. Serve with Yuca Fries (page 65) or the Citrus Jicama Salad (page 47) for a perfect picnic or game day.

YIELDS 24 SLIDERS
Prep Time: 5 MINUTES
Cook Time: 10 MINUTES
Total Time: 15 MINUTES

24 Hawaiian rolls or pão doce (2 packages)
1 to 2 pounds sliced deli ham
9 slices Swiss cheese
24 dill or bread-and-butter pickle slices
8 tablespoons (1 stick) unsalted butter, melted
2 tablespoons finely chopped onion, or 1 teaspoon onion powder
2 tablespoons Dijon mustard

1. Preheat the oven to 350°F.

2. Slice the packaged clump of rolls in half, crosswise, without separating the bottoms from the other bottoms or the tops from the other tops.

3. In a 9-by-13-inch baking dish, place the still-joined bottoms in a single layer.

4. Layer the ham, cheese, and pickles over the bottoms, then top with the still-joined tops.

5. In a small bowl, stir together the butter, chopped onion, and mustard.

6. Pour the butter mixture over the rolls and use a pastry brush to coat evenly.

• To make ahead of time, follow the instructions through Step 4. Cover with foil and refrigerate. When ready to cook, resume with Step 5.

• Wrapped in foil and refrigerated, the sliders will stay fresh for 3 days. To save for later, allow them to cool completely, wrap in plastic wrap, and then again in aluminum foil. Freeze and enjoy within 3 months. To serve, remove the foil and plastic wrap and let thaw to room temperature. Bake in a 350°F oven for 5 minutes, or until the cheese remelts.

7. Cover with aluminum foil and bake until the cheese melts, about 10 minutes.

8. Use a metal spatula or knife to divide the sliders into individual portions, transfer to a serving platter, and serve warm.

VARIATIONS

• If you can't find Hawaiian rolls, use potato rolls or Parker House rolls.

• Add salami, roast pork, or both for meatier sliders. If you like it cheesy, add an extra layer of cheese.

• You can transform these sandwiches into club sliders. After layering the ham, cheese, and pickles, add another layer of roll bottoms; layer with more ham, cheese, and pickles; add the top halves; and bake as directed.

Citrus Jicama Salad

Jicama originated in Mexico, and archaeologists have discovered traces of it in Peru as far back as 3000 BC. It belongs to the legume family, and the name comes from the Nahuatl word for the plant: *xicamatl*. With a thick brown skin, only the root is edible, often eaten raw in salads or dipped in spices, such as Tajín (see Note on page 38). It has a relatively neutral flavor and starchy sweetness, like barely there apple, which makes it the perfect costar for this refreshing, hydrating salad best served cool or chilled.

SERVES 4
Prep Time: 15 MINUTES
Total Time: 15 MINUTES

SALAD

2 jicamas
2 small grapefruits
2 blood oranges
12 ounces radicchio

DRESSING

½ bunch cilantro
1 Jalapeño pepper
2 limes
¼ cup extra-virgin olive oil

TOPPINGS

¼ cup *requesón* or crumbled queso fresco
¼ cup roasted pistachios
Salt

1. Make the salad: Peel and julienne the jicamas, and peel and slice the grapefruits and oranges, carpaccio style.

2. In a large serving bowl, layer the radicchio, grapefruit and orange slices, and jicama.

3. Make the dressing: Chop the cilantro, seed and chop the Jalapeño, and juice the limes.

4. In a blender, blend the Jalapeño pepper, cilantro, lime juice, and olive oil until smooth.

5. Dress the salad, top with the cheese and pistachios, and sprinkle with salt to taste.

TIPS

• To make radicchio less bitter, cut it up and soak it in ice water for 30 minutes. Drain and dry with paper towels.

• To roast raw pistachios, preheat the oven to 350°F and spread the pistachios evenly on an unlined baking sheet. Spray them lightly with cooking oil and sprinkle with salt. Bake until fragrant, 5 to 10 minutes, shaking them halfway through. Transfer to a plate to cool.

Huevos Diablos

Deviling may sound sinister, but it just means making bland food spicy with the addition of peppers, mustard, or similar ingredients. The history of deviled eggs dates back thousands of years. Ancient Romans often ate boiled eggs prepared with zesty sauces as appetizers. The earliest surviving recipe for deviled eggs comes from the Andalusia region of Spain in the 1200s and looks pretty much how we eat them now: Boil and halve the eggs; mix the yolks with cilantro, pepper, onion, a proto–Worcestershire sauce, oil, and salt; put the yolk mixture back in the boiled whites; *y ya está*. The first recipe to include mayonnaise in the mix comes from *The Boston Cooking-School Cook Book* by Fannie Farmer, published in 1896. The following version revisits the dish's Spanish roots with manzanilla olives instead of dill and Latin American *sazón* in place of paprika.

SERVES 6
Prep Time: 10 MINUTES
Cook Time: 10 MINUTES
Total Time: 20 MINUTES

6 large eggs

FILLING
1 tablespoon mayonnaise, plus more if needed
1 tablespoon mustard
½ to 1 teaspoon Sazón (page 197), plus more for dusting
8 manzanilla olives

1. In a medium lidded saucepan, cover the eggs with cold water by 1 inch. Bring the water to a boil, cover, remove from the heat, and set aside for 8 to 10 minutes.

2. While the eggs boil and cook, make the filling: In a small bowl, combine the mayonnaise, mustard, and sazón.

3. Chop the olives, add them to the filling mixture, and set aside.

4. When the eggs have finished cooking, transfer them immediately to an ice water bath. Let them chill for 10 minutes.

5. When the eggs have cooled, peel them, then halve them lengthwise.

6. Scoop out the boiled yolks, add them to the filling mixture, and mash and stir with a fork until fully combined. If the mixture is too dry, add a little more mayonnaise for moisture.

7. Place the egg white halves, cut side up, on a plate or serving tray and scoop roughly 1½ tablespoons of filling into each half egg.

8. Dust them with more sazón to taste, chill for an additional 5 to 10 minutes, if desired, and serve.

Guava Pistachio Baked Brie

From the days of the Roman Empire, Iberians transformed quince—a relative of apples and pears—into a rich, sweet paste eventually called *membrillo* in Spanish and *marmelada* in Portuguese, from which the English word *marmalade* comes. During the colonial period, Brazilians substituted guavas for quince to create *goiabada*. This simple yet satisfyingly gooey recipe uses the tropical flavors of goiabada to riff on baked Brie en croûte. Brie, a soft cheese with a bloomy rind, hails from the Brie region of France, southeast of Paris. Deliciously creamy, it commonly consists of cow's milk but can come from goat's milk, too. The tang of the cheese complements the sweetness of the guava paste, which makes a nice change from the berry or fig jams typically found alongside melted Brie. The pistachios give Brie *al horno* or Brie *assado* a gratifying crunch.

SERVES 8 TO 10
Prep Time: 5 MINUTES
Cook Time: 20 MINUTES
Total Time: 25 MINUTES

One 8-ounce tube crescent rolls
8 ounces Brie cheese
⅔ cup guava paste
⅔ cup chopped pistachios

1. Preheat the oven to 375°F.

2. With a rolling pin, roll the crescent roll dough into a 12-inch square.

3. Place the cheese in the center of the dough. Spread ⅓ cup of the guava paste over it and top with ⅓ cup of the pistachios.

4. Fold the dough around the cheese, trim the excess, and pinch the edges to seal.

5. On an unlined, ungreased baking sheet, place them seam side down.

6. Cut the remaining ⅓ cup of guava paste into cubes and arrange them atop the pastry.

7. Bake for 15 minutes.

8. Top with the remaining ⅓ cup pistachios and return the pan to the oven. Bake until the dough puffs and turns golden brown, about 10 more minutes. Serve warm.

San Antonio Puffy Tacos

According to lore, Maria Rodríguez Lopez—grandmother to brothers Ray, Arturo, Louis, and Henry Lopez, one more brother, and five sisters—accidentally overfried a tostada, which puffed up and folded in half. Not wanting to waste food, she went with it, and her grandsons turned the mishap into American food culture with a fascinating family history. In 1956, Ray Lopez opened Ray's Drive Inn in San Antonio. His younger brothers worked in the kitchen, making the family's signature *crispy* tacos. In the 1960s, Henry and Louis opened El Taco Food to Go, also serving crispy tacos. When Arturo and his own growing family moved to Southern California, Henry closed Taco Food to Go and joined his brother in the Golden State. Planning another family restaurant, Arturo and Henry agreed on *puffy* tacos, and they opened Arturo's Puffy Taco in La Habra, nine miles north of Disneyland, in 1977, followed by locations in Whittier and West Covina. In 1978, Henry returned to San Antonio and opened Henry's Puffy Tacos. In 1982, Arturo also came back to Alamo City, buying Ray's Drive Inn from his older brother and making puffy tacos the signature dish. The US Patent Office granted Arturo a trademark for the puffy taco in 1992, but expensive legal squabbles among the brothers convinced him to abandon it. Now everyone can enjoy this delicate food by name. The first time I saw one, it looked like a hard taco shell had suffered an allergy attack. "It's a taco with . . . *lips*?" I asked. Greasy and chewy, the shell resembles Navajo fry bread, a *salbute*—a lightly fried tortilla—or a *gordita inflada* (literally "puffy, chubby one"), common in Veracruz. It should have an airy crunch, an effect that doesn't last long, so make the fillings first and eat the finished dish quickly.

YIELDS 4 TACOS
Prep Time: 5 MINUTES
Cook Time: 20 MINUTES
Total Time: 25 MINUTES

FILLING
1 medium yellow onion
2 tablespoons vegetable oil
2 cloves garlic
1 pound 80/20 ground beef
Salt
⅔ cup low-sodium beef or
   chicken broth
1 large tomato
Fresh cilantro for garnish
1 cup Refried Beans (page 230)
6 ounces panela cheese, crumbled
12 pickled Jalapeño pepper slices
1 cup shredded iceberg lettuce

SHELL
Vegetable or canola oil for frying
4 uncooked Corn Tortillas (page 210)
Salt

CONTINUES →

1. Make the filling: Chop the onion.

2. In a large skillet over medium-high heat, heat the oil and cook the onion until it softens, 5 to 7 minutes.

3. Meanwhile, mince the garlic.

4. To the skillet, add the garlic, ground beef, and salt. Crumble the meat with a wooden spoon and cook until it browns, 5 to 7 minutes. Drain the excess grease.

5. Add the broth. Lower the heat to low and simmer until the sauce thickens slightly, 2 to 3 minutes. Remove from the heat.

6. Fry the shells: In a deep skillet or a deep fryer set to 375°F, heat 2 inches of vegetable oil.

7. Add 1 uncooked tortilla to the oil. It will puff immediately.

8. After 5 seconds, use tongs, a spider skimmer, or a slotted metal spoon to flip the tortilla. Cook on the other side for 5 more seconds.

9. Fold the fried tortilla in half by gently pressing down the middle with the spider skimmer or slotted spoon. Hold for 10 seconds until the shape keeps.

10. Return the folded taco to the oil and continue flipping, 5 seconds at a time, for 30 more seconds, or until the shell crisps and turns golden brown.

11. Transfer the taco shell to a paper towel–lined plate to drain and season with salt to taste.

12. While the taco shells fry, seed and chop the tomato and chop the cilantro.

13. To assemble the tacos, spoon ¼ cup of refried beans into each shell, followed by one-quarter of the beef mixture, one-quarter of the cheese, 3 Jalapeño pepper slices, ¼ cup of shredded lettuce, and one-quarter of the tomatoes.

14. Garnish with chopped cilantro to taste and serve warm.

Colorado Burritos

I'm what sociologists call a third-culture kid, meaning that I grew up in a society other than my parents', living in a different culture for a meaningful part of my childhood. I was born in Panama City, where my mother later married a German American from Denver, whom the US Navy had deployed to the Canal Zone. His job whisked us all over the world to various military bases. While we were living in Japan, he ordered monthly shipments of canned green chile sauce that he used to make this dish. The green goo smothered the bean-filled flour tortilla, inside and out. It tasted unexpectedly delicious. Don't mistake these for cheese-smothered burritos made with *chiles colorados*, meaning "reddish," nor Denver-style breakfast burritos containing eggs and peppers. I often wonder how my life might have differed if my family had stayed in Panama. Who would I have become? I disliked Husband #2, but without him in my life, I likely never would have discovered this delicious Rocky Mountain burrito.

SERVES 4

Prep Time: 5 MINUTES
Cook Time: 25 MINUTES
Total Time: 30 MINUTES

1 tablespoon vegetable oil
½ teaspoon minced garlic
¼ cup diced sweet yellow onion
8 ounces 80/20 ground beef
⅓ teaspoon Adobo (page 196)
8 ounces Refried Beans (page 230)
One 4- or 7-ounce can green
    chile peppers
Cooking spray
5 or 6 burrito-size Flour Tortillas
    (page 215)
1 cup sour cream
1 cup finely shredded Mexican cheese
½ cup diced Roma tomatoes

1. In a large skillet over medium heat, sauté the oil, garlic, and onion until the onion softens and becomes translucent and fragrant, 3 to 5 minutes.

2. Add the ground beef and crumble it with a wooden spoon.

3. Add the adobo and cook until the meat browns, 7 to 10 minutes.

4. Add the refried beans and half of the green chiles and continue to cook for 5 minutes.

5. While the meat and beans are cooking, prepare the tortillas: Spray a large skillet with cooking spray and place it over medium heat. Warm the tortillas until slightly golden brown, 2 to 3 minutes on each side.

6. To assemble the burritos, lay 1 tortilla on a flat, clean surface. Add 2 tablespoons of the meat mixture down the center, followed by 2 tablespoons of the sour cream, 2 tablespoons of the cheese, and 2 teaspoons of the diced tomatoes.

7. Fold the left and right sides of the tortilla over the filling, then roll tightly, from the bottom up, over the filling.

8. Repeat with the remaining burritos and serve hot.

Fritados Pie

In 1932, Gustavo Olguin placed an ad in the *San Antonio Express*, selling an original recipe for fried corn chips, a modified potato ricer, and 19 retail accounts. (If your Spanish is rusty, *frito* means "fried.") At the same time, Charles Doolin wanted to add something salty to the menu of his family's sweet shop in Alamo City. Doolin bought Olguin's small business for $100, naming it the Frito Company. Over the next few decades, the company expanded its offerings, including Cheetos in 1948, and franchised nationwide. The first recipe to combine Frito-brand corn chips with chili appeared in 1949. Doolin's mother, Daisy, or his secretary, Mary Livingston, may have created it, but the company gave official credit to Nell Morris, who joined Frito in the 1950s and assembled a company cookbook. Frito invested early in Disneyland and established the Casa de Fritos Restaurant there, which sold Frito Chili Pie when the theme park opened in 1955 and created Doritos in the following decade. In 1961, Frito joined forces with the Lay potato chip company to become Frito-Lay, which four years later merged with Pepsi-Cola to become one of the world's largest agribusinesses. New Mexicans assert that Teresa Hernández invented the dish in the 1960s when working at the lunch counter of the Woolworth's in Santa Fe. Whichever version you choose, you can serve this recipe—still popular in the Southwest, Midwest, and Southeast—in a casserole dish for Mexican Casserole (page 114) or as a single serving in a corn chip bag, which gives the dish the name of the Walking Taco in the Midwest.

SERVES 6 TO 8

Prep Time: 5 MINUTES
Cook Time: 30 MINUTES
Total Time: 35 MINUTES

1 small white or yellow onion

1 pound 80/20 ground beef

2 tablespoons Taco Seasoning (page 198)

One 10-ounce can diced tomatoes with green chiles

One 15-ounce can ranch-style beans or pinto beans

1 cup corn, fresh or frozen

One 10¼-ounce bag Fritos

2 cups grated Cheddar cheese

¼ cup chopped green onions

1 cup sour cream

1 cup guacamole of choice (pages 200–203) chilled

1. Preheat the oven to 350°F. Finely chop the onion.

2. In a large skillet over medium-high heat, cook the ground beef and onion until the meat browns and the onion softens, 7 to 10 minutes. Drain any excess grease.

3. Add the taco seasoning, diced tomatoes, beans, and corn and mix until well combined.

4. In a 9-by-13-inch baking dish, spread three-quarters of the Fritos into a single layer. Over the Fritos, spread the chili mixture in an even layer, followed by the cheese.

5. Bake until the cheese melts and bubbles, 15 to 20 minutes.

6. Top with the remaining Fritos, green onions, sour cream, and guacamole.

NOTES

• You can find ranch-style beans in most grocery stores.

• If you want or wind up with leftovers, Fritos get soggy, so when eating the leftovers, crumble a few fresh ones on top for a hearty crunch.

Dominican Spaghetti

One hot summer day, while I was sunning myself on one of New York City's beaches, Dominican families near me were eating spaghetti from pots and plastic containers. Spaghetti as beach food? My curiosity prompted me to find out more and hope for a taste. Over the centuries, Italians immigrated to many Latin American countries, particularly Argentina and Brazil, which absorbed aspects of the European cuisine into their own food cultures. Spaghetti came to the Dominican Republic with Italian migration in the late 1800s. In the 1950s, dictator Rafael Trujillo Molina popularized it by opening Molinos Dominicanos, the island nation's first pasta factory. Pasta proved cheaper than most other foods at the time, so Dominicans eagerly adopted spaghetti, making it their own. They added salami, *salchicha*, *pollo guisado*, and other less expected ingredients, such as corn and evaporated milk, thereby creating a new dish called *espaguetis dominicanos*. Dominican immigrants brought the dish to America, New York City in particular, often enjoying it at beaches or lakeside. White rice or tostones usually accompany the dish, which alternatively can become a sandwich with the addition of *pan de agua* or *pan sobao*. Traditionally the spaghetti and rice are transported in and served from the same pots in which they cooked.

SERVES 8 OR MORE
Prep Time: 5 MINUTES
Cook Time: 35 MINUTES
Total Time: 40 MINUTES

1 or 2 bay leaves
1 pound salami
1 green or red bell pepper
2 cloves garlic
1 onion
1 pound dried spaghetti
2 tablespoons olive oil
¼ cup pitted green olives with the brine
1 tablespoon capers
¾ cup tomato sauce
¾ cup tomato paste
¼ teaspoon dried oregano
⅝ cup evaporated milk
1 teaspoon granulated sugar
1 teaspoon Adobo (page 196)
1 teaspoon Sazón (page 197)
Grated Parmesan cheese
Freshly ground black pepper

1. Fill a large pot with ½ gallon of water, add the bay leaves, and bring to a boil.

2. While the water heats, start the sauce: Cube the salami, seed and chop the bell pepper, mince the garlic, and dice the onion.

3. When the water boils, cook the spaghetti until slightly softer than al dente, 10 to 12 minutes.

4. While the spaghetti cooks, continue the sauce: In a large skillet over medium heat, cook the oil and salami until the meat browns, stirring occasionally, 5 to 7 minutes.

5. Lower the heat to medium-low. Add the onion, garlic, bell pepper, olives and brine, and capers and stir until the onion becomes translucent, 3 to 5 minutes.

6. When the spaghetti finishes cooking, drain, reserve the bay leaves for the sauce, and set aside.

7. To the skillet, stir in the tomato sauce, tomato paste, and oregano.

8. Lower the heat to low and simmer for 3 to 5 minutes.

CONTINUES →

Ah, the great bay leaf debate. Does it do anything? When making pasta, I always toss it into my boiling water—just in case.

9. Stir in the milk, sugar, adobo, and sazón and cook for 5 more minutes.

10. Using tongs, mix the cooked spaghetti in the skillet to coat it thoroughly in the sauce.

11. Top with grated cheese and black pepper to taste and serve with pan sobao or pan de agua.

VARIATION
To turn this delicious culture combination into a spaghetti sandwich, just layer a few forkfuls of pasta between slices of pan de agua or pan sobao.

American Tacos

If you spurn Taco Bell for inauthenticity, keep reading. A variety of crispy tacos—*tacos dorados, taquitos, flautas*, etc.—existed in Mexico for a long time. In Texas, German immigrants wrapped sausages in tortillas, an early convergence of Mexican and "American" cuisines. References to hard-shell tacos in Texas and California date to the 1890s, and Bertha Haffner Ginger mentions deep-fried tacos in her *California Mexican-Spanish Cookbook*, published in 1914. The signature U shape probably came from a tostada gone awry, as with Maria Rodríguez Lopez in San Antonio (page 52). Fabiola Cabeza de Baca Gilbert first described that shape in *The Good Life: New Mexican Food*, published in 1949, and the next year the US Patent Office awarded a patent for a machine to make hard-shell tacos to Juvencio Maldonado, owner of the Xóchitl restaurant in New York City. In 1952, Glen Bell Jr., a hot dog vendor, opened Taco Tia in San Bernadino, California, noting long lines across the street for the tacos dorados sold by Salvador and Lucia Rodriguez at Mitla Café, which he copied. After opening a handful of Taco Tia locations, Bell sold them, started another mini chain called El Taco in Long Beach, sold those, and opened the first Taco Bell in Downey in 1962, which, in the segregated '60s, introduced many white Americans to Mexican food for the first time. The other "classic" ingredients in an American taco—ground beef, Cheddar cheese, iceberg lettuce, tomatoes—come down to availability. As with so many migrating people and cuisines, this taco adapts a Mexican dish to ingredients readily available in America.

SERVES 6

Prep Time: 15 MINUTES
Cook Time: 25 MINUTES
Total Time: 40 MINUTES

12 Corn Tortillas (page 210)
2 cloves garlic
1 medium white onion
2 tablespoons vegetable or olive oil
1 pound ground 80/20 beef
Salt
¼ cup Taco Seasoning (page 198)
⅔ cup low-sodium beef or
   chicken broth
6 ounces panela cheese, crumbled
24 slices pickled Jalapeño peppers
1 cup shredded iceberg lettuce
1 cup Pico de Gallo (page 199)
½ cup chopped fresh cilantro
   leaves (optional)

1. Preheat the oven to 350°F.

2. Roll out a long sheet of aluminum foil. Loosely fold it over itself so it stands about 2 inches high and fold the ends over. It should resemble the shape of a rolling pin. Repeat with 2 or 3 more sheets of foil.

3. On a large baking sheet, place the foil molds.

4. Drape 3 or 4 tortillas over the molds and bake until crisp and firm, about 15 minutes.

5. Repeat with the remaining tortillas.

6. While the tortilla shells bake, make the meat filling: Mince the garlic and chop the onion.

7. In a large skillet over medium-high heat, heat the oil and cook the onion until softened, 5 to 7 minutes.

CONTINUES $\longrightarrow$

VARIATION

You can fry the taco shells instead. In a large cast-iron skillet over medium heat, heat 2 cups of vegetable oil to 350°F, about 5 minutes. Adjust the heat as necessary to maintain the temperature as measured on a deep-fry thermometer. Shape 1 tortilla over the foil mold. Use tongs to hold the sides against the mold and fry the bottom of the tortilla for 20 seconds. Fry one side for 30 seconds, flip over, and fry the other for 30 more seconds. Place the fried shell on a wire cooling rack set over a paper towel–lined baking sheet. Let cool for 30 seconds before removing the mold. Sprinkle the shells with kosher salt to taste. Repeat with the remaining tortillas and keep the shells warm in the oven at 200°F while preparing the filling.

8. Add the garlic, ground beef, and salt. With a wooden spoon, crumble the meat and cook until it browns, 5 to 7 minutes. Drain any excess grease.

9. Add the taco seasoning and broth and simmer until the sauce slightly thickens, 2 to 3 minutes. Remove from the heat.

10. To assemble the tacos, spoon the cooked ground beef into a shell, followed by ½ ounce of crumbled panela cheese, 2 pickled Jalapeño pepper slices, shredded lettuce, 1 heaping tablespoon of pico de gallo, and chopped cilantro (if using).

11. Repeat with the remaining tacos and serve warm.

Taco Pizza

According to a 2022 study by career website Zippia.com, with data sourced from Yelp and Eat24, Iowa's favorite pizza is, you guessed it, taco pizza. Happy Joe's, a pizza chain in Davenport, claims credit for creating the dish when, in 1974, owner Joe Whitty wouldn't let a franchise sell tacos. Instead, Whitty topped a pizza with lettuce, tomatoes, and crumbled taco shells. Casey's, a gas station chain in Iowa, also claims to have invented the dish. In 1979, after securing a handful of state trademarks to the dish, the Pizza Inn chain applied for a national trademark and patent for taco pizza. But Pizza Hut blocked the move by arguing that "taco pizza" represented just a general description, not a special creation. Happy Joe's joined forces with Pizza Hut, and they successfully blocked the trademark and patent. In 1985, Taco Bell added the Pizzazz Pizza to its menu, renaming it Mexican Pizza three years later and proving that good ideas can arise multiple times in various places. Different pizza joints vary the exact ingredients, but they all have refried beans, cheese, and crumbled tortillas in common.

YIELDS 2 PIZZAS (16 SLICES)
Prep Time: 10 MINUTES
Cook Time: 30 MINUTES, PLUS
    COOLING TIME
Total Time: 45 MINUTES

BASE
2 pounds store-bought raw pizza dough
1 pound ground beef
1 ounce Taco Seasoning (page 198)
1 cup water
All-purpose flour for dusting
15 ounces Refried Beans (page 230)
½ cup salsa
2 cups shredded Mexican blend cheese
¼ cup sliced black olives

TOPPINGS
Sour cream
Shredded iceberg lettuce
Jarred or fresh Jalapeño pepper slices
Sliced green onions
Salsa
Corn Tortilla Chips (page 206),
    crumbled or cut into strips

1. Make the pizza base: Preheat the oven to 500°F and remove the pizza dough from the refrigerator.

2. In a large skillet over medium-high heat, crumble the ground beef with a wooden spoon and cook until the meat browns, 7 to 10 minutes.

3. Add the taco seasoning and the water and mix to combine.

4. Lower the heat to low and cook for 10 minutes. Remove from the heat and set aside.

5. On a flat, lightly floured surface, roll out the pizza dough into 2 circles, each 12 inches in diameter.

6. Transfer the dough to 2 large baking or cookie sheets.

7. In a medium bowl, combine the refried beans and salsa.

8. Spread the mixture on the dough, leaving a ½-inch bare border around the outside edges. Top evenly with the shredded cheese and black olives.

9. Bake until the crusts turns golden brown and the cheese has melted, 10 to 15 minutes.

10. Remove the pizzas from the oven and let cool for 5 minutes.

11. Top with sour cream, shredded lettuce, Jalapeño pepper slices, sliced green onions, salsa, and tortilla strips or crumbled chips.

Yuca Fries

Yuca frita comes from cassava and, instead of potatoes, makes excellent fries that, dare I say, taste even better. Also called manioc, the plant originated in Brazil, where Indigenous peoples domesticated it around 10,000 years ago. In the 1500s, the Portuguese brought it from Brazil to Africa at the same time that the Spanish brought it to Asia. Incredibly tolerant of drought, cassava served as an important carbohydrate source in the Americas before the arrival of Europeans and fulfills the same role in developing nations around the world today. It grows in sweet and bitter varieties, and yuca comes from the tuber, while starch extracted from boiling the plant becomes tapioca. These fries are the perfect accompaniment to Latino Fried Chicken (page 93).

SERVES 4

Prep Time: 10 MINUTES
Cook Time: 35 MINUTES
Total Time: 45 MINUTES

Salt
2 pounds yuca, fresh or frozen
2 cups vegetable oil
Chopped fresh cilantro
Cilatro Lime Alioli (page 204) for
 serving

NOTE

These fries also taste great with a mixture of equal parts mayonnaise and ketchup, a popular condiment in Puerto Rico and elsewhere in Latin America.

1. Fill a medium pot with ½ gallon of water, add 1 teaspoon of salt, and bring to a boil.

2. Meanwhile, prepare the yuca: If using fresh, cut off and discard the tops and bottoms.

3. Using a sharp knife, carefully peel the tough skin.

4. Quarter them lengthwise, remove the cores, and wash the quarters in running water.

5. Add the prepared yuca pieces to the boiling water and cook until fork-tender, 20 to 30 minutes. Check midway through by gently pressing a knife or fork against the pieces to see if they give. When done, they should appear translucent, not opaque.

6. With tongs or a slotted spoon, remove the boiled pieces from the pot, shake off the excess water, and transfer them to a paper towel–lined plate.

7. After the pieces have cooled for about 5 minutes, pat them dry, remove any excess fibers, and cut them into smaller strips.

8. In a deep skillet over medium-high heat or a deep fryer set to 350°F, heat 2 inches of oil and fry the pieces until they turn golden, 3 to 4 minutes.

9. Use tongs to remove the fries from the oil and transfer to a cooling rack or a paper towel–lined plate to drain and cool.

10. Sprinkle generously with salt, garnish with chopped cilantro, and serve with cilantro lime alioli.

Collard Greens Empanadas

Empanadas have a long history around the world, but they probably originated in the Galicia region of Spain. Jacob ben Asher—born in Cologne around 1270 and died, a rabbi, in Toledo around 1340—mentions them in *Arba'ah Turim* ("Four Columns"), an important Jewish legal text. In the Age of Exploration, the Spanish Empire eventually controlled the land around the Gulf of Mexico, which in time became Florida ("Flowery"), Alabama, Mississippi, Louisiana, and Texas. This recipe acknowledges that territorial overlap. Mexican food meets the American South in Soul Mex, a culinary convergence centuries in the making. The comfort of Hispanic cuisine finds kinship in the comfort of soul food. Soul recognizes soul. When developing these empanadas, it occurred to me to try transforming them into tamales or to spice them with chipotle and serve them with Mexican red rice. But this recipe for baked finger food feels right, and some southern households—in which Latino influence has filled kitchens, stomachs, and hearts—probably already make collard greens empanadas just like this.

YIELDS 12 EMPANADAS
Prep Time: 10 MINUTES
Cook Time: 35 MINUTES
Total Time: 45 MINUTES

9 ounces collard greens
1 clove garlic
½ medium white onion
3 tablespoons olive oil
6 ounces shredded
　low-moisture mozzarella
3 tablespoons grated Parmesan cheese
3 tablespoons cream cheese
2 teaspoons Smoky Sazón (page 197)
¼ teaspoon kosher salt, plus
　more as needed
¼ teaspoon freshly ground black
　pepper, plus more as needed
1 large egg
1 large egg yolk
12 Empanada Disks (page 227)
Cilantro Lime Alioli (page 204) or
　Queso Blanco (page 208) for serving

1. Roughly chop the collard greens, mince the garlic, and dice the onion.

2. In a large skillet over medium heat, heat the oil until it shimmers. Sauté the onion and garlic until the onion softens, 3 to 5 minutes.

3. Add the collard greens, a few handfuls at a time, stirring between additions. Cook until the greens wilt, about 4 minutes.

4. Lower the heat to low. Stir in the mozzarella, Parmesan, cream cheese, sazón, salt, and pepper and cook until the cheeses melt, about 2 minutes.

5. Remove the pan from the heat. Taste and season with more salt and pepper as desired.

6. Place a rack in the middle of the oven and preheat it to 400°F.

7. Line a rimmed baking sheet with parchment paper or aluminum foil.

8. In a small bowl, lightly whisk the egg with a few drops of water to create egg wash.

9. In another small bowl, lightly whisk the egg yolk.

10. In the center of a dough disk, place 2 tablespoons of the warm filling.

CONTINUES →

11. Brush the egg wash onto the outside edge of the disk. Fold the disk in half over the filling. With your fingers, press the edges to seal, then use the top ½ inch of a fork to seal further. Place the empanada on the lined baking sheet.

12. Repeat with the remaining disks and filling, spacing the empanadas evenly apart on the baking sheet. Brush the whisked egg yolk onto the tops of the raw empanadas.

13. Bake until the empanadas turn golden brown, 20 to 25 minutes.

14. Remove from the oven and let them cool for 5 minutes, then serve with cilantro lime alioli or queso blanco.

San Diego Fish Tacos

The lineage of the fish taco traces back to various Indigenous peoples who fished Mexico's waters and wrapped their catches in corn tortillas. Some evidence indicates that the people of Anahuac, or the Valley of Mexico, ate what we would call tacos filled with fish. Bernal Díaz del Castillo, a conquistador who helped overthrow the Aztec Empire, wrote in his *True History of the Conquest of New Spain* that, in Coyoacán, Hernán Cortés arranged a feast that may have included the dish for his captains. Thousands of years earlier, the Kumeyaay people founded Kosa'aay, the village that became San Diego. In 1542, explorer Juan Rodríguez Cabrillo claimed the surrounding bay for Castile, and 60 years later cartographer Sebastián Vizcaíno named the area for St. Didacus, known in Spanish as San Diego de Alcalá. Four groups of Spanish settlers and missionaries arrived in 1769, and Franciscan priest Junípero Serra y Ferrer founded the mission that year. Fish tacos, as we know them today, come from Baja California State, Mexico. Food lore places their invention in San Felipe on the Gulf Coast or Ensenada on the Pacific in the 1950s. Some say the dish followed the influence of Japanese immigrants, who served beer-batter tempura to locals in the 1920s, but Jews expelled from Spain and Portugal had been making *pescado frito* for centuries. Whatever the origin, Ralph Rubio first tasted fish tacos in Baja California and, taking inspiration, opened Rubio's Fresh Mexican Grill in San Diego in 1983, and from there the fish taco became synonymous with the birthplace of California. See page 52 for more on the history of the taco.

SERVES 6
Prep Time: 15 MINUTES
Cook Time: 30 MINUTES
Total Time: 45 MINUTES

BATTER
1 cup all-purpose flour
2 tablespoons cornstarch
1 teaspoon baking powder
½ teaspoon salt
½ teaspoon freshly ground black pepper
1 large egg
1 cup beer, such as Dos Equis, Modelo, or Tecate

WHITE SAUCE
1 lime
1 Jalapeño pepper
1 tablespoon chopped fresh cilantro
½ teaspoon minced capers
½ cup sour cream
½ cup mayonnaise
½ teaspoon toasted ground coriander
½ teaspoon toasted ground cumin
½ teaspoon dried oregano
½ teaspoon dried dill
¼ teaspoon ground cayenne pepper
¼ teaspoon ground chipotle chile powder

SLAW
3 tablespoons minced red onion
5 cups shredded red or mixed cabbage (one 10-ounce bag)
½ cup chopped fresh cilantro
3 tablespoons apple cider vinegar
1½ teaspoons vegetable oil
½ teaspoon salt

TACOS
Vegetable oil for frying
1 to 1½ pounds skinless cod fillets
2 tablespoons all-purpose flour, plus more as needed
Twelve 6-inch Corn Tortillas (page 210)
Chopped fresh cilantro
Lime wedges for serving

CONTINUES ⟶

1. Make the batter: In a large bowl, whisk together the flour, cornstarch, baking powder, salt, and black pepper.

2. Beat the egg in a small bowl and add the beer.

3. Stir the egg mixture into the flour mixture. You want a few lumps remaining, so don't overmix. Set aside.

4. Next, make the white sauce: Juice the lime, seed and mince the Jalapeño pepper, chop the cilantro, mince the capers, and combine them in a medium bowl.

5. Stir in the sour cream, mayonnaise, coriander, cumin, oregano, dill, cayenne pepper, and chipotle chile powder. The sauce should have a runny consistency. If too thick, add more lime juice. If too watery, add more sour cream. Refrigerate.

6. Now, make the slaw: Mince the red onion.

7. In a medium bowl, toss the cabbage, cilantro, red onion, cider vinegar, oil, and salt to coat evenly, then set aside.

8. In a medium skillet over medium heat or a deep fryer set to 375°F, heat ½ inch of oil.

9. Cut the cod fillets into 1-by-4-inch strips.

10. Working in batches, lightly dust the fish strips first with flour, then dip them into the beer batter. Let excess batter drip off.

11. Fry the fish strips until they become crisp and golden brown, about 2 minutes per side. If using a skillet, don't crowd the strips. Drain on a paper towel–lined plate.

12. While the fish fries, warm the tortillas: Preheat the oven to 350°F.

13. Wrap 2 stacks of 6 tortillas each in aluminum foil and heat in the oven until heated through, about 15 minutes.

14. Divide the fried fish strips equally among the tortillas, then add slaw, drizzle with white sauce, and top with cilantro to taste.

15. Serve warm with lime wedges.

Kogi Kimchi Burritos

When living in Japan, my family often visited South Korea for vacation. When not losing our minds at Lotte World theme park, we explored Korean food and flavors: *bimbimbap, boricha, bulgogi, jjigae,* and of course kimchi. In Los Angeles, Korean and Mexican cuisines have converged beautifully. The connection arose from proximity. LA's Koreatown borders Hispanic-heavy neighborhoods in Mid City, and many Mexicans work in the kitchens of Korean restaurants. In the early 2000s, Roy Choi famously combined the two cuisines, creating the *kogi* barbecue taco. (*Kogi* means "meat" in Korean.) Around 2009, HRD in San Francisco manifested it as a burrito. In 2010, *Food and Wine* magazine named Choi one of its top ten best new chefs, the first food-truck chef to receive that accolade, which drew even more well-deserved attention to his work. But why Korean and Mexican in particular? The flavors differ significantly but still pair nicely. The pungency and acidity of fermented cabbage cut through the creaminess of cheese or aioli. Flour tortillas perfectly support fruity-marinated beef and white rice. Starting in the City of Angels, this unlikely hybrid traveled up the West Coast before spreading across the country and beyond.

SERVES 4
Prep Time: 30 MINUTES
Cook Time: 15 MINUTES
Total Time: 45 MINUTES

MEAT
2 pounds rib-eye steak or top sirloin
1 apple or Bosc, Asian, or Korean pear
4 cloves garlic
3 scallions
1 medium white onion
3 tablespoons light brown sugar
1 teaspoon freshly ground black pepper
⅓ cup soy sauce
3 tablespoons sesame oil
1 tablespoon canola oil

VINAIGRETTE
1 clove garlic
¼ lime
¼ cup rice vinegar
2 tablespoons soy sauce
2 teaspoons fish sauce
¼ teaspoon red pepper flakes

MAYONNAISE
¼ cup mayonnaise
2 tablespoons sriracha

BURRITO
1⅓ cups uncooked white rice
1⅓ cups water
¼ cup fresh cilantro
¼ cup fresh mint
4 Flour Tortillas (page 215)
⅔ cup kimchi
½ cup grated Cheddar or Monterey Jack cheese
1 cup baby spinach

CONTINUES ⟶

1. Prepare the meat: Thinly slice the meat and place in a large bowl or large plastic storage bag. Set aside.

2. Peel and roughly chop the apple and roughly chop the garlic, scallions, and half of the onion.

3. Slice the remaining onion half and set aside.

4. In a blender or food processor, blend or process the chopped onion, garlic, scallions, apple, brown sugar, black pepper, soy sauce, and sesame oil until smooth.

5. Pour the marinade over the beef, add the sliced onion, and mix to coat evenly. Cover the bowl or seal the bag and marinate in the refrigerator for at least 30 minutes or up to overnight.

6. While the meat marinates, prepare the vinaigrette: Crush the garlic clove and juice the lime.

7. In a small bowl, combine the crushed garlic, lime juice, rice vinegar, soy sauce, fish sauce, and red pepper flakes. Let rest for at least 30 minutes.

8. Make the mayonnaise: In another small bowl, stir together the mayonnaise and sriracha.

9. When ready to make the burritos, combine the rice and water in a rice cooker and cook according to the manufacturer's instructions to yield a little over 3 cups of cooked rice.

10. While the rice cooks, remove the meat from the marinade and pat dry with paper towels.

11. In a large skillet over high heat, heat the canola oil and sear the beef until browned, 5 to 7 minutes. Set aside.

12. Chop the cilantro and mint and set aside.

13. In a large, dry skillet over medium-low heat, warm the tortillas for about 30 seconds per side or use heatproof tongs to heat them over a flame for a few seconds on each side.

14. Plate the tortillas and divide the fillings equally among them: warm rice, chopped herbs, kimchi, cheese, and then meat.

15. Drizzle with the vinaigrette and sriracha mayonnaise.

16. Fold the left and right sides of the tortilla over the filling, then roll tightly, from the bottom up, over the filling. Serve warm.

San Diego Burritos

In the 1950s, Roberto and Dolores Robledo emigrated from San Luis Potosí State, Mexico, to San Diego, California. In 1964, they started a *tortillería* at home and quickly scaled their business, buying several area restaurants and, around 1970, renaming them all Roberto's Taco Shop, one of America's first taco chains. As the chain grew, Robledo hired relatives and friends from San Luis Potosí to run the various restaurants. After a disagreement about making fresh rice and beans daily, one of his cousins renamed that location Alberto's, which launched a series of spin-offs, including Filiberto's, Gualberto's, Hilberto's, Rigoberto's, Ruriberto's, and more. Roberto and Dolores divorced in 1979 but remained business partners, and their 13 children helped run many of the businesses. The San Diego burrito originated at one of the -berto's in the 1980s. Another outstanding example of Cal-Mex cuisine, this classic contains a surprise inside: French fries. Carne Asada Fries (page 80) came about a decade later, but at heart, this dish represents those fries in burrito form, containing no rice or beans. For such an iconic staple of the birthplace of California, it's strange that the first recorded mention of the burrito appears in the *Albuquerque Tribune* in 1995, but that lag in attention doesn't reflect the burrito's or the chain's success. When Robledo died in 1999, Roberto's Taco Shop had 60 locations nationwide.

SERVES 4
Prep Time: 30 MINUTES
Cook Time: 20 MINUTES
Total Time: 50 MINUTES

CARNE ASADA
1 pound skirt or flank steak
Adobo (page 196)
½ lemon
½ lime
1 clove garlic
½ small yellow onion
1½ teaspoons olive oil

BURRITOS
8 ounces frozen French fries
4 Flour Tortillas (page 215)
½ cup Pico de Gallo (page 199)
½ cup guacamole of choice
   (pages 200–203)
Louisiana Hot Sauce (page 225)
½ cup shredded Mexican blend cheese
½ cup sour cream (optional)
Chopped fresh cilantro

CONTINUES ⟶

1. Make the carne asada: Cut the meat into ¼-inch strips, place the strips in a lidded bowl or in a plastic storage bag, and season lightly with adobo.

2. Juice the lemon and lime, mince the garlic, and chop the onion.

3. Add the onion, garlic, and citrus juice to the meat and mix well, gently pressing the marinade into the meat. Cover or seal and refrigerate for at least 30 minutes or up to 24 hours.

4. While the meat marinates, start the burritos: Cook the French fries according to the package directions and have ready the tortillas, pico de gallo, and guacamole.

5. In a medium skillet over medium-high heat, heat the olive oil.

6. With tongs or a slotted spoon, remove one-quarter of the meat from the marinating bowl or bag, allowing any excess marinade to drain off.

7. Sear the meat until it browns on all sides, about 5 minutes.

8. Repeat with remaining meat. Set aside.

9. To assemble the burritos, place one-quarter of the carne asada in the center of a tortilla. Add 2 tablespoons of the pico de gallo, 1 to 2 tablespoons of the guacamole, and a few French fries. Top with hot sauce to taste, 2 tablespoons of the cheese, sour cream (if using), and cilantro.

10. Fold the left and right sides of the tortilla over the filling, then roll tightly, from the bottom up, over the filling. Serve hot.

Mole Fries

The word *mole* comes from the Nahuatl *molli*, which means "sauce," and the mole family contains lots of variations identified by color, ingredients, origins, and other characteristics: *almendrado* (almonds), *amarillo* (yellow), *blanco* (white), *colorado* or *coloradito* (reddish), *manchamantel* (tablecloth stainer), *michoacano* (from Michoacán State), *negro* (black), *pipián* (pumpkin seeds), *poblano* (from Puebla State), *prieto* (dark), *ranchero* (country style), *rojo* (red), *rosa* (pink), *tamaulipeco* (from Tamaulipas State), *tlilmolli* (from Tlaxcala State), *verde* (green), *xiqueño* (from the city of Xico), and more. In his *General History of the Aspects of New Spain*, completed in 1577, Bernardino de Sahagún, a Franciscan friar and missionary who studied Nahuatl extensively, recorded that the Nahua people used mollis on a variety of foods, including vegetables, game, and fish. Indigenous peoples drank chocolate rather than incorporating it into sauces, though, so that now-requisite ingredient entered the mix at a later date, as did cinnamon. The earliest surviving recipes for mole appear in the 1810s. Puebla and Oaxaca States both claim credit for inventing the sauce, with various improbable legends serving as origin stories, but the Poblano version has become the standard-bearer for the family. For more on the history of French fries, see Carne Asada Fries (page 80). In the early 2000s, in Los Angeles, mole joined forces with French fries to create this indulgent, Latino equivalent of poutine.

SERVES 4 TO 6
Prep Time: 10 MINUTES
Cook Time: 45 MINUTES
Total Time: 55 MINUTES

FRIES
24 ounces frozen French fries
1 tablespoon olive oil
1 tablespoon Sazón (page 197)
Pico de Gallo (page 199), sour cream or crema Mexicana, crumbled queso fresco, white sesame seeds, and chopped fresh cilantro for serving

MOLE
3 cloves garlic
1 medium yellow onion
2 tablespoons olive oil
2 teaspoons adobo sauce from canned chipotle peppers
1 teaspoon chili powder
½ teaspoon ground cinnamon
½ teaspoon ground cumin
½ teaspoon dried Mexican oregano
2 tablespoons masa harina

2 cups chicken broth, low-sodium or sodium-free
¼ cup creamy peanut butter
1 tablespoon tomato paste
2 ounces unsweetened Mexican chocolate, such as Abuelita brand
1 teaspoon coarse sea salt
1 teaspoon freshly ground black pepper

VARIATION

To eat them in Alta California style, top the mole fries with braised short ribs.

1. Make the fries: Place a rack in the upper third of the oven and pre-heat it to 425°F.

2. In a large bowl, toss the frozen fries, oil, and sazón to coat evenly.

3. On a large, unlined baking sheet, spread the seasoned fries in a single layer.

4. Bake until they crisp and brown, about 30 minutes.

5. While the fries bake, make the mole: Mince the garlic and chop the onion.

6. In a medium saucepan over medium-high heat, heat the oil and sauté the onion, stirring occasionally, until softened and translucent, about 5 minutes.

7. Add the garlic and adobo sauce and sauté, stirring occasionally, until the garlic becomes fragrant, 1 to 2 minutes.

8. Add the chili powder, cinnamon, cumin, and oregano. Sauté for 1 more minute, stirring occasionally.

9. Remove the pan from the heat and allow the vegetables to cool.

10. In a small bowl, whisk together the masa harina and ¼ cup of the broth until thickened. Set aside.

11. In a blender, blend the cooled vegetables and remaining 1¾ cups of chicken broth until smooth.

12. Transfer the blended mixture to the medium saucepan over medium-high heat. Add the peanut butter, tomato paste, chocolate, salt, and black pepper. Whisk until the chocolate melts and incorporates.

13. Add the masa harina mixture and whisk together. Lower the heat to medium-low and simmer the mole until it thickens, 5 to 10 minutes.

14. Lower the heat to low, stirring occasionally so skin doesn't form.

15. When the fries finish baking, either leave them on the baking sheet or transfer them to a large serving platter.

16. Pour the mole over the fries. Serve with pico de gallo, sour cream or crema Mexicana, crumbled queso fresco, white sesame seeds, and chopped fresh cilantro.

Carne Asada Fries

For such a simple dish, fried potatoes have a surprisingly long pedigree. Indigenous peoples first domesticated the potato, a New World crop, around Lake Titicaca, which straddles the border between southern Peru and northwestern Bolivia. Francisco Núñez de Pineda y Bascuñán, a Chilean soldier who wrote equitably of the Mapuche people, mentioned eating *papas fritas* in 1629, but he didn't give specifics. In the Columbian Exchange, potatoes made their way to Spain, which, like the rest of Europe, had a long history of frying food. President Thomas Jefferson ate "potatoes served in the French manner" in 1802, but, again, we don't know details. Whatever that style, Parisian chefs in the 1840s and '50s modified the traditional French method—presumably into what we recognize today as French fries—and the phrase "french fried potatoes" first appears in English in *Cookery for Maids of All Work* by Eliza Warren, published in London in 1856. The San Diego Burrito (page 75), which contains French fries, arose in the 1980s, and Lolita's Mexican Food claims credit for inventing carne asada ("grilled meat") fries in the 1990s.

SERVES 8
Prep Time: 30 MINUTES
Cook Time: 30 MINUTES
Total Time: 1 HOUR

CARNE ASADA
2 pounds skirt or flank steak
Adobo (page 196)
1 lemon
1 lime
2 cloves garlic
1 small white onion
1 tablespoon olive oil

FRIES
2 russet potatoes
2 tablespoons olive oil
1 teaspoon Adobo (page 196)
1 teaspoon paprika

FOR SERVING
½ cup grated Cheddar cheese
¾ cup Pico de Gallo (page 199)
½ cup guacamole of choice
    (pages 200–203)
¼ cup sour cream or crema Mexicana
½ cup chopped fresh cilantro
1 lime

NOTE

This recipe serves a crowd, so invite loved ones and tell them to come hungry.

1. Make the carne asada: Cut the meat into ¼-inch strips, place the strips in a lidded bowl or in a plastic storage bag, and season lightly with adobo.

2. Juice the lemon and lime, mince the garlic, and chop the onion.

3. Add the onion, garlic, and citrus juice to the meat and mix well, gently pressing the marinade into the meat. Refrigerate for at least 30 minutes or up to 24 hours.

4. While the meat marinates, make the fries: Preheat the oven to 450°F and line a baking sheet with parchment paper.

5. Wash and dry the potatoes and cut them into wedges.

6. In a large bowl, mix the potatoes, olive oil, adobo, and paprika by hand to coat evenly.

7. Place the raw fries on the baking sheet and bake for 12 to 15 minutes.

8. Use a spatula to flip them over and bake until the fries turn crispy and golden brown, 12 to 15 more minutes. Remove from the oven and set aside.

9. Cook the carne asada: In a medium skillet over medium-high heat, heat the olive oil.

10. With tongs or a slotted spoon, remove one-quarter of the meat from the marinating bowl or bag, allowing any excess marinade to drain off.

11. Sear the meat until it browns on all sides, about 5 minutes.

12. Repeat with the remaining meat. Keep warm by covering with a lid or aluminum foil and set aside.

13. To serve, sprinkle the fries with the cheese and top with the carne asada, pico de gallo, guacamole, sour cream, and cilantro.

14. Halve the lime and squeeze one half for 1 tablespoon of juice. Sprinkle over the fries.

15. Quarter the other lime half into wedges for serving.

Cuban Sandwiches

One of the most recognizable dishes of Floribbean cuisine, the Cuban sandwich dates to the mid-1800s, but no one knows its precise origins. In 1885, Vicente Martínez Ybor, who had established cigar factories first in Havana and then Key West, founded Ybor City, a company town outside Tampa, and moved his operations there. The next year, after a fire devastated Key West, an influx of Spanish, Cuban, and Italian immigrants shifted Florida's cigar industry to Ybor City, which Tampa soon annexed into a neighborhood. Around 1900, Ybor City cafés were serving Cuban sandwiches. After the Communist Revolution of 1959, they became common in Miami. Influenced by the large Italian population, Cubans in Tampa use Genoa salami. Cubans in Miami don't. As with anything delicious, it involves a fight. However you slice it, it's a pig of a sandwich: roast pork, ham, and salami in Tampa. The roast pork marinates in *mojo*, a Cuban sauce featuring bitter orange juice, and when made properly the sandwich is assembled on Pan Cubano (page 32). If you do see one there—a product of reverse immigration, like the Puerto Rican *jibarito* (page 106)—it's probably a *mixto*, a combination of different meats.

SERVES 4 TO 6
Prep Time: 30 MINUTES
Cook Time: 30 MINUTES
Total Time: 1 HOUR

ROAST PORK

1 cup bitter (Seville) orange juice

2 tablespoons olive oil

3 cloves garlic

1 teaspoon salt

½ teaspoon freshly ground
    black pepper

½ teaspoon smoked paprika

½ teaspoon ground cumin

1 tablespoon dried oregano

1 pound boneless pork tenderloin

SANDWICHES

3 loaves Pan Cubano (page 32)

8 tablespoons (1 stick) unsalted butter,
    at room temperature

½ cup yellow mustard

½ cup mayonnaise

3 large dill pickles

1 pound sliced honey-glazed ham

6 slices Genoa salami (required for
    Tampa, omit for Miami)

12 slices Swiss cheese

CONTINUES

• Said in my best Ina Garten: To skip a
couple of steps and save time, store-
bought pulled pork or rotisserie-style
pork is fine in lieu of marinating your
own (which of course I recommend).

• If using a skillet to toast the bread,
press firmly with a hard spatula to
flatten the sandwich.

• Instead of pan Cubano, you can use
baguettes or sub bread.

• Many Latino markets sell bitter
oranges (*naranjas agrias*), but if you
can't find them, combine the juice of 1
Valencia or navel orange with the juice
of 2 limes.

1. Preheat the oven to 450°F and line a large baking sheet with 2 layers of foil.

2. Make the roast pork: In a food processor or blender, combine the orange juice, olive oil, garlic, salt, pepper, paprika, cumin, and oregano and process or blend until smooth to make the mojo marinade.

3. In a large bowl, add the pork tenderloin and pour the mojo marinade over it. Cover the bowl with plastic wrap and let marinate on the counter for at least 30 minutes.

4. Transfer the marinated tenderloin to the prepared baking sheet and pour some mojo over it. Discard the remaining marinade.

5. Roast the pork, basting occasionally with the pan juices, until the center reaches 140°F on a meat thermometer, 20 to 25 minutes.

6. Transfer the roast pork to a cutting board and let it rest for 5 minutes.

7. While the meat rests, prepare the rest of the sandwiches: Halve the pan Cubano loaves lengthwise.

8. With a butter knife or soft spatula, spread the butter on the outsides of each loaf, 4 teaspoons per side. Place them, butter side down, on the cutting board.

9. In a small bowl, whisk together the mustard and mayonnaise. Spread 2 heaping tablespoons of the mixture on the inside of each piece of bread.

10. Thinly slice the pickles crosswise.

11. After the meat has rested, carve it diagonally into ¼-inch slices.

12. Layer the bottom slices of bread with the sliced ham, salami if making Tampa style, pickles, roast pork, and cheese, then close the sandwiches.

13. In a large, dry skillet over medium-high heat or a panini press set to 350°F, toast the sandwiches until the bread crisps and the cheese melts, 3 to 4 minutes per side in a skillet or total for a panini press.

14. Cut each sandwich in half diagonally and serve hot.

Mission Burritos

In 1770, Franciscan priest Junípero Serra y Ferrer, following orders from the inspector general of New Spain, led an expedition from Baja California to Alta California to construct a series of missions. From one of those—Misión San Francisco de Asís, established in 1776 by Francisco Palóu and Pedro Cambón to convert the Ohlone people—grew the city of San Francisco. The Mission became one of the city's first neighborhoods and the epicenter of its Hispanic population (until gentrification). In the 1930s, burritos appeared on the menu of El Cholo Spanish Café in Los Angeles, and Erna Fergusson included them in her *Mexican Cookbook*, a collection of New Mexican recipes published in 1934. By the 1950s, the burrito's influence had spread north and west, and the decade after, this variation emerged, traditionally credited to one of two Mexican restaurants in the Mission: Taqueria La Cumbre or El Faro. For this "super" burrito, the tortillas run extra large, a foot in diameter, and steaming helps them stretch to accommodate an impressive volume of fillings tightly rolled shut. You'll recognize it at Chipotle, the fast-food chain founded by Steve Ells in Denver in 1993, who took inspiration directly from the Mission burrito.

SERVES 4
Prep Time: 30 MINUTES
Cook Time: 35 MINUTES
Total Time: 1 HOUR 5 MINUTES

CARNE ASADA
1 pound skirt or flank steak
Adobo (page 196)
½ lemon
½ lime
1 clove garlic
½ medium white onion
1½ teaspoons olive oil

BEANS
3 tablespoons lard, vegetable
  shortening, or vegetable oil
One 15-ounce can pinto beans
Salt

BURRITOS
4 Flour Tortillas (page 215)
1 cup shredded Monterey Jack cheese
Mexican Rice (page 218)
1 cup Pico de Gallo (page 199)
¼ cup Salsa Verde (page 226)
1 cup guacamole of choice
  (pages 200–203)
½ cup sour cream or crema Mexicana

CONTINUES ⟶

• If you make the beans and rice ahead of time, rewarm both on low heat with 1 to 2 tablespoons of water until it absorbs, about 3 minutes.

• Making your own flour tortillas will allow you to achieve a larger diameter, which suits these huge burritos. If you opt for store-bought, use the largest tortillas that you can find, often labeled "burrito-size" in grocery stores.

VARIATIONS

• For the Mexican rice, you can substitute Cilantro Lime Rice (page 209).

• For a Mission burrito dorado, lightly grease a skillet and cook the burrito, seam side down, until it browns, 1 to 2 minutes. Flip and repeat on the other side.

1. Make the carne asada: Cut the meat into ¼-inch strips, place the strips in a lidded bowl or in a plastic storage bag, and season lightly with adobo.

2. Juice the lemon and lime, mince the garlic, and chop the onion.

3. Add the onion, garlic, and citrus juice to the meat and mix well, gently pressing the marinade into the meat. Cover or seal and refrigerate for at least 30 minutes or up to 24 hours.

4. In a medium skillet over medium-high heat, heat the olive oil.

5. With tongs or a slotted spoon, remove one-quarter of the meat from the marinating bowl or bag, allowing any excess marinade to drain off.

6. Sear the meat until it browns on all sides, 7 to 10 minutes.

7. Repeat with the remaining meat. Keep warm by covering with a lid or aluminum foil and set aside.

8. Next, make the beans: In a small lidded pot over medium-low heat, heat the lard, add the drained pinto beans, and cook, covered, stirring occasionally, until the beans warm through, about 10 minutes.

9. Salt the beans to taste, remove from the heat, and set aside.

10. To assemble the burrito, first warm a tortilla. Lightly brush it with water and place, wet side down, in a large pan over medium heat. Cook until it softens and the water has evaporated.

11. Brush the other side with water, flip the tortilla, and sprinkle ¼ cup of the cheese over it. Cook until the cheese melts and the water has evaporated.

12. Transfer the tortilla to a flat surface. Down the center, spoon a layer of rice, beans, more cheese, the carne asada, and one-quarter each of the pico de gallo, salsa verde, guacamole, and sour cream.

13. Fold the left and right sides of the tortilla over the filling. Tightly wrap the bottom over the filling and tuck it in, then roll the burrito away from you onto the top part of the tortilla. Wrap in foil.

14. Repeat with the remaining tortillas and fillings.

Esquites Herb Salad

The word *esquites* comes from the Nahuatl word *ízquitl*, which means "toasted corn," and Nahua tradition attributes the creation of the dish to the god Tlazocihuapilli of the Xochimilca people. Today, vendors traditionally serve this creamy, spiced *antojito* (Mexican street food) in a cup, which gives it the English name "corn in a cup." The dish features ingredients from Europe and the Americas, making it a popular bridge for non-Mexican folks to try Mexican food. Similar to *elote*, eaten off the cob, esquites typically contain mayonnaise, Cotija cheese, lime juice, chili powder, and, in some Mexican states, epazote, a pungent herb reminiscent of anise and oregano. Traditionally it's eaten hot or warm, but this cold update makes room for fresh spring veggies.

SERVES 4 TO 6
Prep Time: 5 MINUTES
Cook Time: 30 MINUTES, PLUS
    COOLING TIME
Total Time: 1 HOUR 30 MINUTES

3 cloves garlic
½ small white onion
3 tablespoons unsalted butter
5 ears corn
5 cups water
2 or 3 sprigs epazote
½ teaspoon kosher salt, plus
    more to taste
½ lime
⅓ cup finely chopped basil leaves
½ cup finely chopped scallions, green
    parts only
½ ounce fresh cilantro leaves,
    finely chopped
½ cup Cotija cheese
½ cup crema Mexicana
½ cup mayonnaise
½ teaspoon freshly ground
    black pepper
Chili powder

1. Finely chop the garlic and onion.

2. In a large skillet over medium-high heat, heat the butter and cook the garlic and onion until the onion becomes translucent and fragrant, 5 to 7 minutes.

3. Meanwhile, shuck the corn and, with a kernel stripper or knife, strip off the kernels.

4. Add the corn to the skillet and cook for 3 to 5 more minutes.

5. Add the water, the epazote, and salt. Boil until the corn softens, about 20 minutes.

6. Let cool to room temperature, transfer to a large bowl, cover, and refrigerate for 30 minutes.

7. When ready to serve, juice the ½ lime for roughly 1 tablespoon of juice and add to the corn mixture along with the basil, scallions, and cilantro.

8. Add the cheese, crema, mayonnaise, salt to taste, and black pepper and toss well to combine.

9. Dust with chili powder to taste and serve.

VARIATIONS

• Mix in your favorite spring veggies, such as chopped blanched asparagus, spring peas, snap peas, or edamame.

• Instead of or in addition to the basil, add a little fresh mint.

Texas Chili con Carne

Never put beans in your chili con carne. It's called "chili" because it contains chiles, and it's *con carne*, not *con frijoles*. At its heart, the dish consists of beef chunks and a spice blend in (beer) broth, all cooked low and slow until tender. Franciscan friar and missionary Bernardino de Sahagún recorded in the 1500s that people in Tenochtitlan, Mexico City today, ate chile stew. The Spanish adapted it by adding beef. Two centuries later, King Felipe V of Spain ordered a group of families to relocate from the Canary Islands to San Fernando de Béjar, now San Antonio, to limit the growth of French Louisiana. In La Villita, those families made a thick stew of meat, cumin, garlic, chile peppers, and onions. From around 1850, Everette DeGolyer, a chili enthusiast, discovered records of chili bricks—beef, fat, chile peppers, and salt—dried for reconstituting into a field stew, and the phrase *chile con carne* first appears in 1857 as the title of a book by S. Compton Smith about his experiences in the Mexican-American War. In the 1880s, William Tobin, formerly a Texas Ranger, arranged to sell canned goat chili to the US armed forces, and in San Antonio, the chili queens, a group of enterprising Latinas, were selling chili stew to soldiers in Military Plaza and then Market Square. At the 1893 Columbian Exposition in Chicago, the San Antonio Chili Stand brought the dish to a national audience, and a year later William Gebhardt, a German immigrant who lived in New Braunfels and ran the Phoenix Café, introduced the first commercial chili powder, called Tampico Dust. Ken Finlay's song "If You Know Beans about Chili, You Know That Chili Has No Beans" came along in 1976, and the next year, Texas declared chili the state food.

SERVES 5 TO 6
Prep Time: 10 MINUTES
Cook Time: 2 HOURS
Total Time: 2 HOURS 10 MINUTES

SPICE BLEND
2 teaspoons whole coriander seeds
1½ teaspoons whole cumin seeds
2 tablespoons masa harina
1 tablespoon ancho chile powder
1 teaspoon dried Mexican oregano
1½ teaspoons smoked paprika
1½ teaspoons chipotle chile powder
½ cup hot water

CHILI
2 pounds stew meat, chuck roast, or steak
Salt
1 tablespoon canola oil
2 Jalapeño peppers, plus 1 or more for serving
3 cloves garlic
½ large white onion
1½ teaspoons Worcestershire sauce
6 ounces dark lager
½ ounce unsweetened dark chocolate
1 or 2 large whole dried guajillo peppers
1 quart water

FOR SERVING
Corn Tortilla Chips (page 206)
Sour cream or crema Mexicana
Pico de Gallo (page 199)
Chopped fresh cilantro

CONTINUES ⟶

The chili will taste best 1 or 2 days after you make it. To reheat it, set a large skillet over medium-high heat and cook the chili for about 10 minutes, stirring occasionally to prevent scorching. If it's too thick, stir in 1 tablespoon of water at a time until it achieves the desired consistency.

VARIATIONS

• For more depth of flavor, you can replace some of the quart of water with more beer or brewed coffee.

• Instead of ancho chile powder, pasilla or Chimayo also work.

• If you don't have unsweetened chocolate, substitute 1 tablespoon of unsweetened cocoa powder in the spice blend.

1. Make the spice blend: In a small, heavy, dry skillet over medium-high heat, toast the coriander and cumin seeds until fragrant, about 30 seconds. Occasionally shake the skillet to prevent scorching.

2. With a coffee/spice grinder, mortar and pestle, or molcajete (page 201), grind them to a powder.

3. In a medium bowl, combine the coriander-cumin powder with the remaining dry spice blend ingredients, then mix with the hot water to form a paste. Set aside.

4. Make the chili: Roughly cut the beef into 2-inch cubes or slice it against the grain into pieces 1½ inches square by ¼ inch thick. Sprinkle with salt.

5. In a large, heavy pot over medium-high heat, heat the canola oil until it shimmers.

6. Brown the meat, turning occasionally, until it turns crusty, 7 to 10 minutes. Drain on a paper towel–lined plate.

7. While the meat cooks, mince the Jalapeño peppers and garlic and dice the onion.

8. In the same heavy pot, use a wooden spoon to loosen any brown bits. Add 1 more tablespoon of oil, if necessary, followed by the onion, garlic, Jalapeños, and the spice paste. Stir to coat the meat thoroughly.

9. Cook, stirring occasionally, until the onion softens, about 5 to 10 minutes.

10. Add the cooked meat, Worcestershire sauce, lager, chocolate, guajillo peppers, and the water.

11. Lower the heat to low and simmer until the meat becomes fork-tender, about 1½ hours. Remove the guajillos. Taste and add salt, if necessary.

12. Serve immediately with corn tortilla chips, sour cream or crema Mexicana, Jalapeño pepper slices, pico de gallo, and fresh cilantro, or let cool to room temperature and refrigerate.

Latino Fried Chicken

Thousands of years ago, Southeast Asians domesticated a jungle bird into the chicken, which spread via ancient trade routes to the Middle East, Africa, and Europe. Many of those cultures developed similar ways to cook it, including frying. More recently, Scots fleeing the Highland Clearances, which began in 1760, relocated to other parts of the British Empire, including the American South. Those immigrants brought with them a tradition of eating chicken fried but with no seasoning. Many of them and their descendants enslaved laborers captured or descended from West African peoples, who had their own traditions of frying chicken with various seasonings. The first known recipe for fried chicken appeared in *The Art of Cookery Made Plain and Easy* by Hannah Glasse, published in London in 1747, and the first American recipe for it appeared in *The Virginia House-Wife* by Mary Randolph, published in 1824. Psyche Williams-Forson, a James Beard Award–winning food historian, identified Gordonsville, Virginia, as the place where, starting in the 1850s, black women popularized the distinctly American version of the dish by selling it to train passengers. But Latino cultures have their own iterations, of course. This recipe proves particularly popular in Central America. Before the Pollo Campero fast-food chain came stateside and outsold Nashville hot chicken, people flying from Guatemala and El Salvador often brought as much chicken as possible. Southerners have embraced this dish as well. Even if you have no ties to Central America, it will satisfy a deep, emotional craving for comfort food for the soul.

SERVES 4
Prep Time: 1 HOUR 30 MINUTES
Cook Time: 45 MINUTES
Total Time: 2 HOURS 15 MINUTES

MARINADE
4 cloves garlic
4 limes
2 teaspoons dried oregano
2 teaspoons Sazón (page 197)
1 tablespoon ground cumin
1 tablespoon kosher salt
1½ teaspoons freshly ground
    black pepper

COATING
2 cups all-purpose flour
2 tablespoons cornstarch
1 tablespoon Adobo (page 196)
1 tablespoon freshly ground
    black pepper
1 teaspoon ground cumin
1 teaspoon kosher salt
¼ teaspoon cayenne pepper

CHICKEN
8 pieces chicken (4 drumsticks,
    4 thighs), skin on, bone in
Canola or vegetable oil for frying

FOR SERVING
Yuca Fries (page 65)
Cilantro Lime Alioli (page 204)
Pico de Gallo (page 199)
Lime wedges

CONTINUES $\longrightarrow$

• For the crispiest, juiciest chicken, buy skin-on, bone-in meat. The skin provides a better surface for the marinade and coating to adhere.

• Shaking off the excess marinade before coating also yields better results because the drier the skin, the crispier when cooked.

• Reheat leftovers on an unlined baking sheet in a 300°F oven for 8 to 10 minutes.

TIPS

• If not using a deep fryer, attach a candy or deep-fry thermometer to your Dutch oven to confirm the oil temperature.

• To check the chicken for doneness, insert a meat thermometer into the thickest part, without touching bone, to confirm that the internal temperature reaches or exceeds 165°F.

• For the best fried chicken, make sure the oil temperature returns to 350°F before frying the next batch.

1. Make the marinade: Mince the garlic and juice the limes.

2. In a small bowl, whisk together the lime juice, garlic, oregano, sazón, cumin, salt, and black pepper.

3. Marinate the chicken: In a large lidded bowl or a gallon-size plastic storage bag, add the chicken pieces, pour in the marinade, and massage to coat thoroughly. Cover or seal and refrigerate for at least 1 hour and up to 2 hours.

4. Meanwhile, make the coating: In a large bowl, whisk together the flour, cornstarch, adobo, pepper, cumin, salt, and cayenne.

5. Remove the marinated chicken from the refrigerator. Allow any excess marinade to drain and remove any solids, such as large pieces of garlic.

6. Dredge the chicken in the coating mixture, coating well on all sides. Transfer coated pieces to a clean plate or a wire rack atop a baking sheet to rest for 10 to 15 minutes.

7. Meanwhile, in a large Dutch oven over medium-high heat or a deep fryer set to 350°F, heat 2 to 3 inches of frying oil for about 15 minutes.

8. Using tongs, gently lower 2 or 3 pieces of chicken into the oil and fry, rotating the pieces with tongs every 3 to 4 minutes, until golden brown, 12 to 15 minutes. The center of the meat should reach an internal temperature of at least 165°F.

9. When done frying, place the pieces on a cooling rack over a paper towel–lined baking sheet.

10. Repeat to fry the rest of the chicken.

11. Let the fried chicken rest for 10 minutes and serve with yuca fries, cilantro lime alioli, pico de gallo, and lime wedges.

VARIATIONS

• Instead of or in addition to legs and thighs, you can use wings.

• In a pinch, lemons can work in lieu of limes.

• For extra-crispy chicken, substitute 1 cup of rice flour or rice starch for the all-purpose flour in the coating mixture.

• If you don't like the fiery heat of cayenne pepper, omit it or swap out for something milder, such as chili powder or paprika.

• If you don't want to make or buy adobo, use garlic and/or onion powder.

New Orleans Hot Tamales

In Central America, tamales date back many thousands of years. Various Indigenous peoples ate them—including the Olmecs, Toltecs, Aztecs, and Mayas—for religious and other celebratory purposes. Spanish conquistadores, including Álvar Núñez Cabeza de Vaca and Hernando de Soto, explored the area around the Mississippi River Delta but never controlled it. In 1718, Jean-Baptiste Le Moyne de Bienville of France's Compagnie d'Occident (Western Company) founded the colony of La Nouvelle-Orléans. In 1762, during the French and Indian/Seven Years' War, France secretly yielded New Orleans and the Louisiana territory to Spain. In 1800, King Carlos IV and Napoléon Bonaparte signed a secret agreement returning Louisiana to France. Three years later, President Thomas Jefferson's administration bought the Louisiana territory for $15 million. Born in Mexico, Manuel Hernández started selling his special hot tamales in New Orleans in 1933, and they quickly gained popularity. They started in corn husks, but he transitioned them to wrappers made of parchment paper. In 1968, Hernández's son-in-law inherited the family business, which sadly didn't survive the devastation of Hurricane Katrina in 2005. But you can enjoy a version of them here. Unlike Mexican tamales, New Orleans tamales don't use corn husk wrappers. Another adaptation of Mexican food absorbed into Soul Mex cuisine, cornmeal, rather than masa harina, goes into the raw-meat filling, and it all cooks together as a uniform mixture in a pot of tomato water.

YIELDS 50 SMALL TAMALES
Prep Time: 30 MINUTES
Cook Time: 2 HOURS
Total Time: 2 HOURS 30 MINUTES

BOILING SAUCE
8 ounces tomato sauce
¼ teaspoon chili powder
1 teaspoon ground cumin
Salt and freshly ground black pepper

FILLING
2 medium white onions
½ cup water
4 ounces tomato sauce
2 teaspoons coarse salt
1½ teaspoons cayenne pepper
1½ teaspoons garlic powder
½ teaspoon freshly ground
    black pepper
½ teaspoon ground cumin
¼ cup chipotle chile powder
½ teaspoon smoked paprika
¾ cup yellow or white cornmeal, plus
    more for rolling
1½ pounds ground beef chuck

1. Make the boiling sauce: In a small pot over medium-high heat, bring the tomato sauce to a boil, then stir in the chili powder, cumin, and salt and black pepper to taste.

2. Lower the heat to low and simmer for 3 minutes. Remove from the heat and set aside.

3. While the sauce simmers, begin the filling: Quarter the onions.

4. In a blender or food processor, blend or process the water, tomato sauce, onion, coarse salt, cayenne, garlic powder, black pepper, cumin, chipotle chile powder, paprika, and cornmeal until smooth.

5. In a large bowl, place the beef and pour the processed filling mixture over it. Wearing food-grade gloves, thoroughly combine the beef and filling mixture by hand.

6. On a sheet of parchment paper or a cutting board, roll 1 to 2 tablespoons of the filling into an oblong shape.

7. In the center of a tamal paper, foil rectangle, or coffee filter, place the oblong filling. Fold the sides over and then the ends.

8. In a large lidded stockpot, place the wrapped tamal flat.

9. Repeat Steps 6 through 8 with the rest of the filling, keeping each layer of tamales flat in the stockpot and aligned in the same direction, then alternating the direction of the next layer.

10. Place the stockpot over medium heat, cover the tamales with water, add the boiling sauce, cover, and bring to a boil.

11. Lower the heat to low and simmer for 2 hours.

12. With tongs, remove the tamales from the water and plate them on a serving dish. Let them rest for 5 minutes before serving.

VARIATION

For even more heat, increase the cayenne pepper to taste.

Dinner

Cena

Jantar

Philly Cheesesteak Quesadillas

In 1930, brothers Pat and Harry Olivieri ran a hot dog stand in South Philadelphia's Italian Market. According to family history, they invented the steak sandwich in 1933 and sold the first one to a taxi driver. In 1940, they opened Pat's King of Steaks, which has become a Philadelphia icon. The original sandwich didn't contain cheese, though, which Joe Lorenza added later. Puerto Ricans make up the lion's share of Philly's Latino population, but Mexicans have joined them in small waves, particularly after the North American Free Trade Agreement went into effect in 1994. El Centro de Oro and South Philly have become hubs of Latino culture, and Mexican Philadelphians have helped revitalize the city and given the historic Italian Market the nickname Puebladelphia. The mixing of cultures has led to delicious innovation, such as *quesabirria* ramen, this dish, and more.

SERVES 2
Prep Time: 5 MINUTES
Cook Time: 15 MINUTES
Total Time: 20 MINUTES

1 pound rib eye or top round beef
8 ounces mushrooms
1 red bell pepper
½ large yellow onion
Adobo (page 196)
1 tablespoon vegetable oil
1 clove garlic
6 slices American cheese
2 burrito-size Flour Tortillas (page 215)

TIP
For a crisper tortilla, add a little oil to the pan in Step 9.

1. Slice the beef into thin strips. Quarter the mushrooms. Slice the bell pepper into thin strips. Cut the onion into half rings.

2. Lightly season the beef and vegetables with adobo.

3. In a large skillet over high heat, heat the oil and sauté the vegetables until golden brown, 5 to 7 minutes.

4. Meanwhile, mince the garlic.

5. Add the garlic to the pan and cook until fragrant, about 30 seconds. Remove the vegetables from the skillet and set aside.

6. Add the beef strips to the skillet and sauté until browned, 7 to 10 minutes.

7. Return the vegetables to the skillet and stir to combine. Top with half of the cheese slices and let the mixture rest for 1 minute so the cheese melts.

8. Halve the filling and add each portion to the side of each of the tortillas. Top the filling with the rest of the cheese. Fold the tortillas in half.

9. Return the skillet to medium heat and sauté the quesadillas until the cheese melts, about 2 minutes. When the bottom becomes golden and crispy, flip it and cook for 1 to 2 more minutes.

10. Slice into wedges and serve.

Los Angeles Street Dogs

These dogs go by many names: LA hot dogs, Mission dogs, and, in San Diego, Tijuana dogs. The dish draws inspiration from Sonoran hot dogs, which arose in Hermosillo, the capital of Sonora State, Mexico, in the 1980s. They have become extremely popular in Tucson (245 miles north of Hermosillo), Phoenix, and much of southern Arizona. Bolillos are best, but you can sub hot dog buns in a pinch. *Dogueros* typically serve them with a fried güero on the side and a splash of Jalapeño hot sauce.

SERVES 4
Prep Time: 5 MINUTES
Cook Time: 15 MINUTES
Total Time: 20 MINUTES

4 beef hot dogs

4 slices bacon

4 güero chiles or banana peppers, plus more for serving

1 medium tomato

½ small yellow onion

4 bolillos

½ cup Refried Beans (page 230)

Mayonnaise, ketchup, mustard, and Salsa Verde (page 226) for serving

1. Over medium heat, set a lidded grill pan or cast-iron skillet.

2. While it heats, wrap each hot dog completely with a slice of bacon and secure each with a toothpick.

3. Cook the bacon dogs, covered, rotating them every minute with tongs, until the bacon crisps and the hot dogs cook through, 5 to 7 minutes.

4. While the hot dogs cook, place the peppers in a small, dry skillet over medium heat and cook for 3 to 6 minutes, flipping them occasionally to char all sides. Remove from the heat.

5. While the peppers char, dice the tomato and chop the onion.

6. Steam the bolillos by wrapping them loosely in paper towels and microwaving them on low (30 to 50% power) until soft and warm, 7 to 10 seconds.

7. In a microwave-safe bowl, microwave the beans on high until steaming, 2 to 3 minutes, stirring them every minute.

8. Into each roll, spread 2 tablespoons of refried beans.

9. Place the cooked bacon dog in the roll and top with 1 tablespoon of onion and 2 tablespoons of tomato.

10. Serve with mayonnaise, ketchup, mustard, salsa verde, and more güero chiles or banana peppers.

Chimichangas

Various stories compete for crediting the origin of this deep-fried burrito popular in Southwestern and Tex-Mex cuisines, but they all take place in Mexican restaurants in Arizona. In one version, Monica Flin, owner of El Charro Café in Tucson, accidentally dropped a burrito in hot oil, shouting what became the name of the dish in lieu of a proper expletive. According to Francisco Santamaría's *Diccionario de Mejicanismos*, published in 1959, *chivichanga* meant "thingamajig" in Tabasco State. Another story credits Woody Johnson—owner of Woody's El Nido (later Macayo's Mexican Kitchen) in Phoenix—with inventing it on purpose in 1946. Delicious either way.

SERVES 6
Prep Time: 5 MINUTES
Cook Time: 15 MINUTES
Total Time: 20 MINUTES

Canola or vegetable oil for frying
2 cloves garlic
1 medium white or yellow onion
2 tablespoons olive oil
½ teaspoon dried Mexican oregano
1 teaspoon toasted and ground cumin
1 teaspoon chili powder
1 teaspoon salt
2½ cups shredded rotisserie chicken or cooked chicken breast
2 cups Refried Beans (page 230)
1½ cups Pico de Gallo (page 199)
1 cup shredded Mexican blend cheese
6 Flour Tortillas (page 215)
Salsa Roja (page 217), Salsa Verde (page 226), guacamole of choice (pages 200–203), Queso Blanco (page 208), and sour cream for serving

1. In a Dutch oven or deep fryer set to between 375° and 400°F, heat 4 inches of canola oil.

2. While the oil heats, mince the garlic and chop the onion.

3. In a medium skillet over medium-high heat, heat the olive oil and cook the onion and garlic until softened, about 3 minutes.

4. Meanwhile, crush the Mexican oregano.

5. To the skillet, add the oregano, cumin, chili powder, and salt. Cook, stirring, for about 30 seconds. Stir in the chicken and refried beans.

6. Remove from the heat and stir in the pico de gallo and cheese.

7. Place ½ cup of filling in the center of each tortilla. Fold the left and right sides of the tortillas over the filling, then roll tightly, from the bottom up, over the filling. Secure them with wooden skewers or toothpicks.

8. Using tongs or a spider skimmer, place 2 chimichangas in the hot oil and fry until golden brown, 2 to 3 minutes. Transfer to a paper towel–lined plate to drain and cool.

9. Repeat with the remaining chimichangas.

10. Remove the skewers or toothpicks and serve the chimichangas on a bed of shredded iceberg lettuce along with salsa, guacamole, queso blanco, sour cream, and more pico de gallo.

VARIATIONS

• Make it vegetarian by swapping out the beef for Mexican Rice (page 218).

• For baked chimichangas, preheat the oven to 450°F and coat a baking sheet with cooking spray or butter. Follow Steps 2 through 9. Spray the chimichangas with cooking spray or coat them lightly in more butter, place them seam side down on the baking sheet, and bake for 8 to 10 minutes per side.

Loaded Nachos

A bowling alley, that's where I first ate nachos. Superfake liquid cheese sauce smothered stale chips, and I loved them because I didn't know any better—yet. My tastes evolved just like the prevailing recipe for the dish. See page 42 for the simple origins of nachos. From there, they've reached new heights with lots of toppings and endless variations. Ignacio Anaya created the original, but Frank Liberto of San Antonio receives credit for the runny orange cheese that we know and love at bowling alleys, fairs, movie theaters, sporting events, and more. His family's company supplied concessions for games at Arlington Stadium, where the Texas Rangers played baseball. In 1976, he created shelf-stable, liquid cheese that he could make faster than melting Colby and Cheddar. Crowds loved it, and sports commentator Howard Cosell mentioned the dish a number of times in 1978, popularizing it with sports fans nationwide. There's no wrong way to make loaded nachos, so here's my way.

SERVES 4 TO 6

Prep Time: 5 MINUTES

Cook Time: 25 MINUTES

Total Time: 30 MINUTES

½ medium yellow onion

1 pound 80/20 ground beef or shredded rotisserie chicken

2 tablespoons Taco Seasoning (page 198)

¾ cup water

16 ounces Corn Tortilla Chips (page 206)

2 cups Refried Beans (page 230)

8 ounces Cheddar cheese, grated

8 ounces Monterey Jack cheese, grated

6 ounces pickled Jalapeño peppers, or 2 to 3 fresh

2 to 3 green onions

½ cup guacamole of choice (pages 200–203)

½ cup sour cream

½ cup Salsa Roja (page 217) or Salsa Verde (page 226)

1. Preheat the oven to 400°F, line 2 baking sheets with parchment paper or foil, and dice the onion.

2. In a medium skillet over medium-high heat, crumble the meat with a wooden spoon, and cook the meat and onion until the meat browns and the onion softens and becomes translucent, 5 to 7 minutes. Drain any excess grease. If using shredded rotisserie chicken, add it halfway through cooking the onion.

3. Add the taco seasoning and the water. Bring the water to a boil, lower the heat to low, and simmer until the liquid mostly evaporates, about 5 minutes.

4. While the seasoned meat cooks, place the tortilla chips in a single layer on unlined baking sheets.

5. Spoon the refried beans onto the chips, followed by the cooked meat, and sprinkle the cheeses on top.

6. Bake until the cheeses melt, 5 to 10 minutes.

7. While the nachos bake, slice the Jalapeño peppers, if using fresh, and the green onions.

8. Top the cooked nachos with guacamole, sour cream, salsa, Jalapeños, and green onions and serve.

Chicken Jibarito BLTs

The ways that food travels can prove fascinating, particularly reverse immigration. In Maracaibo, Venezuela, a sandwich with fried plantains (tostones or patacones) instead of bread is a *patacón maracucho*. In the Dominican Republic, it's just a *patacón*. In Aguada, Puerto Rico, Jorge Muñoz and Coquí Feliciano served a similar dish at Plátano Loco, their restaurant, in 1991. Juan Figueroa, who owned the Borinquen Restaurant in Chicago, read about the Plátano Loco sandwich and created his own version in 1996, Americanizing it with lettuce, tomatoes, cheese, more mayonnaise than a *patacón*, and garlic oil. He called it a *jibarito*, which means "little bumpkin." It instantly became an iconic dish. After New York City, Chicago has the second-largest population of Puerto Ricans outside Puerto Rico, and word spread. Now islanders enjoy it, too, and with this recipe, so can you.

YIELDS 2 SANDWICHES
Prep Time: 5 MINUTES
Cook Time: 35 MINUTES
Total Time: 40 MINUTES

GARLIC OIL
¼ lime
½ head garlic
½ cup olive oil
1½ teaspoons white vinegar
Salt

SANDWICH
2 unripe green plantains
Canola, corn, or vegetable oil for frying
2 slices American cheese
4 slices bacon
1 tomato
4 sprigs cilantro
2 cups shredded roasted chicken or
    protein of choice
½ cup mayonnaise, plus more
    for smearing
1 avocado
4 leaves romaine lettuce
Adobo (page 196)

1. Make the garlic oil: Juice the lime and mince the garlic.

2. In a small saucepan over low heat, combine all the garlic oil ingredients, including salt to taste, and cook for 5 minutes. Don't let the garlic burn. Remove from the heat and set aside to cool.

3. Next, prepare the plantains for the sandwich. Cut off the ends and slit the thick skins lengthwise. Remove the peels and halve the plantains crosswise.

4. In a heavy-bottomed skillet, Dutch oven, or deep fryer set to 350°F, heat 1 inch of frying oil and fry 2 plantain halves at a time until they turn golden brown, 3 to 4 minutes per side. With a spider skimmer or slotted metal spoon, transfer them to a paper towel–lined plate to drain and cool while keeping the oil at 350°F in the cooking vessel.

5. On a flat surface, lay a sheet of plastic wrap or a large plastic storage bag and use a pastry brush to oil it lightly.

6. When the plantains have cooled enough to handle, place 1 plantain half on one side of the plastic. Fold the other half of the plastic over the plantain. Working slowly, gently press the plantain with a flat-bottomed plate until the fruit flattens to ¼ inch thick.

7. Repeat with the remaining plantain halves.

CONTINUES →

TIP
Drizzle the extra garlic oil over Yuca Fries (page 65) or dip chunks of Pan Cubano (page 32) in it.

8. Return the flattened plantains to the cooking vessel and fry until they turn golden brown and crisp, about 3 to 4 more minutes on each side. With a spider skimmer or slotted metal spoon, transfer them to a paper towel–lined plate to drain and cool.

9. Place 2 cheese slices atop 2 flattened and fried plantain slices, 1 on each, allowing their residual heat to melt the cheese.

10. While the plantains cool, fry the bacon, 2 minutes per side.

11. Meanwhile, slice the tomato, chop the cilantro, and slice the avocado.

12. In a small bowl, combine the chicken and mayonnaise and halve the mixture.

13. Spread each portion of chicken salad on each of the cheese-topped plantain halves, then layer each with half of the sliced tomato, half of the avocado, 2 bacon slices, and half of the cilantro.

14. Smear the remaining plantain halves with a little mayonnaise.

15. Place the mayo-smeared plantain halves, mayo side down, atop the filled plantain halves, then brush the top of each sandwich with garlic oil and lightly sprinkle with adobo to taste.

16. Cut each sandwich in half, if desired, and serve.

VARIATIONS

• The *jibarita* (feminine spelling) uses sweet, ripe plantains.

• Instead of garlic oil, you can use garlic butter by combining 1 tablespoon of melted butter with ¾ teaspoon of roasted minced garlic.

• You also can mix the chicken with garlic mayonnaise (aioli) and omit the extra smear of mayo and garlic oil—or, better yet, amp it up. Mix ¾ cup of mayonnaise, 3 minced garlic cloves, 2½ tablespoons of fresh lemon juice, ¾ teaspoon of salt, and a few grinds of black pepper.

• Instead of mayo chicken, you can use 10 ounces of sliced chicken breast, roast pork from the Cuban Sandwich (page 82), steak, tuna, or your protein of choice.

• For a vegetarian sandwich, omit the chicken and bacon.

Chili Mac

I first ate this American dish with Mexican roots on a military base in Japan. Introduced to the military menu in 1995, it's a favorite meal, ready-to-eat (MRE) among enlisted officers, though it comes unceremoniously in a bland beige pouch. Some diners in St. Louis, Missouri, serve a version of this cozy comfort food topped with fried eggs, called chili mac à la mode.

SERVES 6

Prep Time: 20 MINUTES
Cook Time: 35 MINUTES
Total Time: 55 MINUTES

2 tablespoons olive oil

10 ounces dried elbow pasta

1 green bell pepper

1 red bell pepper

1 medium yellow or white onion

1 pound 80/20 ground beef, chicken, or turkey

2 tablespoons Taco Seasoning (page 198)

1 cup canned black or kidney beans

26 ounces diced tomatoes (1 large can)

3 cups low-sodium chicken or beef broth

½ cup evaporated milk

2 cups grated Mexican cheese

Chopped green onions for garnish

1. Preheat the oven to 375°F.

2. In a large lidded skillet or Dutch oven over medium heat, heat 1 tablespoon of the olive oil, add the uncooked pasta, and toast until golden, 2 to 3 minutes. Remove from the pan.

3. Meanwhile, seed and chop the bell peppers and chop the onion.

4. To the same skillet over medium heat, add the remaining 1 tablespoon of oil and the ground beef, onion, and bell peppers. Crumble the beef with a wooden spoon and cook until the meat browns and the vegetables soften, about 5 minutes. Drain the excess grease.

5. Add the taco seasoning, lower the heat to low, and simmer, stirring occasionally, for 5 minutes.

6. Meanwhile, drain and rinse the beans.

7. Stir in the rinsed beans, tomatoes, broth, and toasted pasta.

8. Bring the liquid to a boil, lower the heat to low, cover, and simmer until the pasta is al dente, 9 to 12 minutes.

9. Add the evaporated milk and 1 cup of the grated cheese. Stir to combine and melt.

10. Sprinkle the remaining cheese on top. Cover again, just until the cheese melts, about 1 minute.

11. Garnish with the green onions.

Tamal Pie

Around the turn of the 20th century, tamal pie probably originated in Texas. The inspiration for it likely came from Mexico's *tamal de cazuela*, a traditional dish from Yucatán State that you shouldn't confuse with Cuba's *tamal en cazuela* or Panama's *tamal de olla*. *Tamal* is singular, *tamales* are plural. Now you know.

SERVES 8
Prep Time: 20 MINUTES
Cook Time: 40 MINUTES
Total Time: 1 HOUR

FILLING

2 cloves garlic

1 medium yellow or white onion

1 tablespoon extra-virgin olive oil

1 teaspoon ground cumin

1 teaspoon ancho chili powder

Salt and freshly ground black pepper

1 pound ground beef

1 tablespoon sauce from canned chipotle chile in adobo

⅓ cup Salsa Roja (page 217) or red enchilada sauce

1 cup shredded Cheddar cheese

1 cup shredded Monterey Jack cheese

CORNBREAD

1 cup cornmeal

½ cup all-purpose flour

2 teaspoons baking powder

1 teaspoon kosher salt

1 large egg

½ cup sour cream

½ cup creamed corn

1. Preheat the oven to 375°F.

2. Mince the garlic and chop the onion.

3. In a large cast-iron skillet over medium heat, heat the olive oil and cook the onion, cumin, chili powder, and salt and black pepper to taste until the onion softens, about 5 minutes.

4. Add the garlic and cook it until it becomes fragrant, about 1 minute.

5. Add the ground beef, breaking it up with a wooden spoon, and cook until browned, about 6 minutes. Drain the excess grease.

6. Stir in the chipotle chile sauce and salsa roja and set aside.

7. In a small bowl, combine the cornmeal, flour, baking powder, and salt.

8. In another small bowl, whisk together the egg, sour cream, and corn.

9. Add the dry mixture to the wet mixture and stir to combine into a batter.

10. Fold the cheeses into the meat mixture or sprinkle them on top.

11. Using a soft spatula, dollop the cornbread batter onto the beef filling and spread it into an even layer.

12. Bake until the pie turns golden and a skewer inserted into center of the cornbread comes out clean, about 20 minutes.

13. Remove from the oven, let cool for 5 minutes, slice, and serve with sour cream and cilantro.

TIP
You can make the beef filling ahead of time and refrigerate it in its sauce for up to 2 days.

Cuban Pizza

No one knows for sure when *pizza Cubana* originated. Some say it started in the 1930s, when a large wave of Italian immigrants came to the island. But we know that it came from Havana or Varadero to Miami in the 1980s. So what makes it Cuban? It runs about 1 inch thick when baked; a molten bed of cheese also covers the crust; a little sugar goes into the dough and sauce; and of course there are distinctly Caribbean toppings, listed below. You can fold it and eat it like a sandwich, NYC-style, and if you want it at a restaurant, order it *picada*, the Cuban way of saying "sliced."

SERVES 1
Prep Time: 45 MINUTES
Cook Time: 15 MINUTES
Total Time: 1 HOUR

DOUGH

One ¼-ounce packet active dry yeast (2¼ teaspoons)
1 teaspoon granulated sugar
1 cup warm water (about 110°F)
2½ cups all-purpose flour
½ teaspoon salt
1 tablespoon extra-virgin olive oil, plus more for bowl, pan, and rolled-out dough

TOPPINGS

⅓ cup pizza sauce
1 teaspoon granulated sugar
½ cup shredded Gouda cheese
½ cup shredded mozzarella cheese

VARIATIONS
Optional additional Cuban toppings include bell peppers, chorizo, ham, *lechón asado*, pepperoni, picadillo, shrimp, and sweet plantains.

1. Make the dough: In a small bowl, whisk together the yeast, sugar, and 1 cup of warm water. Let sit until the yeast activates (bubbling and foaming), 5 to 10 minutes.

2. In a medium bowl, stir together the flour, salt, olive oil, and yeast mixture with a wooden spoon until the dough just comes together.

3. Knead the dough until it becomes soft and elastic, about 5 minutes.

4. Oil a bowl, place the dough in it, cover the bowl with plastic wrap, and let rise until doubled in size, about 30 minutes.

5. While the dough rises, preheat the oven to 450°F and oil a cookie sheet or pizza stone with olive oil.

6. Place the dough on the prepared cookie sheet or pizza stone and gently roll or stretch it into a 9-inch-diameter circle.

7. With a toothpick or fork, poke holes in the surface of the dough. Using a pastry brush, brush the top of the dough with more olive oil.

8. Make the toppings: Stir the sugar into the pizza sauce and then spread it evenly onto the dough.

9. In a small bowl, combine the cheeses.

10. If topping only with cheese, cover the entire pizza with it, including the crust. If using additional toppings (see variations), halve the shredded cheeses, put one portion over the sauce and crust, add the toppings, and top with the other portion of cheese.

11. Bake until the cheese melts and the crust turns golden brown, 10 to 15 minutes.

12. Transfer to a cutting board, slice with a pizza cutter, and serve.

Mexican Casserole

People have been making casseroles for ages, but the conventions solidified in the 1870s. The tradition originated in France, and the word means "little pan" in French. Early versions consisting mostly of rice and meat branched off into French cassoulets, British potpies, and so on. The category has flexible rules. Ingredients generally mix in a bowl and cook in a baking dish. Many contain a creamy element, a protein and/or vegetable (usually canned), and a typically crunchy top layer. But what distinguishes a casserole from other baked dishes, such as, say, lasagna? The casserole dish and simple, accessible, economical ingredients assembled with minimal skill. In America, casserole cooking peaked in the 1950s with food company research and development. But as a comfort food, they remain popular in the Midwest, where they ease the bite of cold winters. When my family lived overseas, visitors who hailed from the Midwest often shared their favorite casseroles with us. But of course Latino cooking has casseroles, too. *Pastel azteca*, a traditional Mexican dish, is a tortilla casserole, and Puerto Rico and the Dominican Republic have *pastelón*, made with plantains. Influenced by Mexican cuisine, many Californians love a good tamal casserole. This dish riffs on the Fritados Pie (page 56), which midwesterners casseroled with tortilla chips instead of corn chips. You can use those or Doraditos (page 207) if you like.

SERVES 10 TO 12

Prep Time: 5 MINUTES

Cook Time: 1 HOUR

Total Time: 1 HOUR 5 MINUTES

1 red bell pepper

1 pound 80/20 ground beef

One 16-ounce can chili beans

One 4.5-ounce can diced green chiles

One 2-ounce can sliced black olives

6 Corn Tortillas (page 210)

2 tablespoons Taco Seasoning (page 198)

2 cups Salsa Roja (page 217) or Salsa Verde (page 226)

Cooking spray

½ cup chopped green onion

½ cup chopped tomato

2 cups shredded Mexican or Cheddar cheese

2 cups sour cream

¼ cup chopped fresh cilantro

1. Chop the bell pepper.

2. In a large skillet over medium-high heat, add the ground beef and bell pepper, crumble the beef with a wooden spoon, and cook until it browns and the pepper softens, 8 to 10 minutes.

3. Meanwhile, drain the chili beans, green chiles, and olives and use a pizza cutter to slice the tortillas into halves.

4. Add the taco seasoning to the skillet and stir to coat the beef and vegetables.

5. Add the salsa and green chiles, lower the heat to low, and simmer until the liquid absorbs, about 20 minutes.

6. Meanwhile, preheat the oven to 350°F.

7. Add the beans to the skillet and cook until they heat through, about 5 minutes.

8. Spray a 9-by-13-inch baking dish with cooking spray and arrange half of the tortilla halves in it.

9. To the baking dish, evenly add half of the beef mixture and sprinkle with the olives, green onions, and tomatoes. Cover with half of the cheese.

10. Repeat with the remaining tortilla halves, beef mixture, and cheese.

11. Bake until hot and bubbly, about 30 minutes. Remove from the oven, top with the sour cream, and garnish with cilantro.

Chicken and Cheese Tamales with Salsa Verde

Tamales have a long lineage, dating to the Olmecs and Toltecs of ancient Mexico. In his *General History of the Aspects of New Spain*, Bernardino de Sahagún, a Franciscan missionary and one of the first anthropologists, recorded the wide variety of tamales eaten in the Aztec Empire in the 1500s. Centuries later, each Latin American country fills, wraps, and cooks tamales differently. Panamanians use banana leaves, while Mexican tradition calls for corn husks, as in this recipe—and that's just the beginning. Tamales spread from Mexico to Texas and then the rest of the American South. In 1893, the Chicago World's Fair introduced them to a national audience. Today, you can buy them on New York City street corners, and different American states have their own variations: Arkansas Delta Tamales (page 121), New Orleans Hot Tamales (page 96), Texas tamales, and more. Nothing tastes as good as a homemade tamal (the correct singular), but they're a labor of love. All that work means that people usually make them only around the Christmas holidays at a *tamaladas* (a tamal-making party). You have to participate if you want to eat the results, so don't hesitate to ask for help in the kitchen when making these.

YIELDS 20 TO 25 SMALL TAMALES
Prep Time: 30 MINUTES
Cook Time: 3 HOURS
Total Time: 3 HOURS 30 MINUTES

DOUGH

2 cups lard or vegetable shortening
3½ cups chicken broth
2 tablespoon baking powder
2 tablespoons Sazón (page 197)
1 tablespoon salt
4 cups masa harina

FILLING

2 pounds rotisserie chicken
3 cups Salsa Verde (page 226), plus more for drizzling
16 ounces shredded Oaxaca or Monterey Jack cheese

1. Bring a kettle of water to a boil.

2. While the water heats, rinse 27 corn husks in cold water to remove any debris.

3. In a large heatproof bowl, cover the rinsed husks with the boiling water.

4. Carefully place a heavy plate or other heatproof object on the husks to submerge them completely. Soak for 30 minutes.

5. Meanwhile, start making the dough: In the bowl of a stand mixer fitted with the whisk attachment, whip the lard on medium-high until fluffy peaks form, about 20 minutes. The color will change from yellow to white.

6. Reduce the speed to medium and whip for 5 more minutes.

7. While the lard is whipping, prepare the broth: In another medium bowl, whisk together the broth, baking powder, sazón, and salt.

CONTINUES ⟶

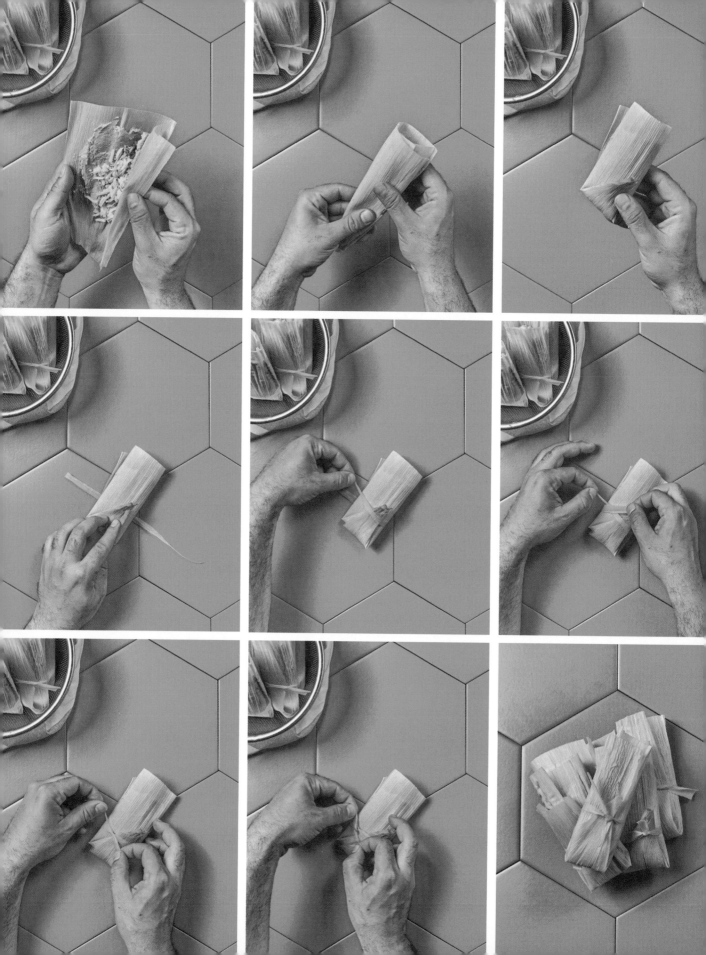

8. Working in batches of about ¼ cup, slowly pour the broth mixture into the whipped lard and whip at low to medium until the broth incorporates into the fat. Wait until each batch of broth incorporates completely before adding more. Mix for about 5 minutes.

9. When all the broth has incorporated, switch out the whisk for the flat beater attachment. Add the masa harina, 1 cup at a time, and beat on medium-high speed until the dough becomes smooth, 15 to 20 minutes. Set aside.

10. While the masa is beating, make the filling: Debone the chicken.

11. With the dough bowl removed from the mixer and still using the flat beater attachment, shred the chicken in another bowl of the stand mixer on low speed.

12. In a large saucepan over medium heat, simmer the salsa verde and shredded chicken for 10 minutes. Remove from the heat and let cool for 5 to 10 minutes.

13. While the chicken mixture cools, drain the husks and shake off any excess water.

14. Tear 2 husks lengthwise, with the grain, into ¼-inch-thick strips. Set aside.

15. To the center of a husk, add about 2 tablespoons of the masa (dough).

16. Using the back of a spoon, a soft spatula, or a masa spreader, spread the masa toward the widest part of the husk, leaving a small border, ¼ to ½ inch, all around.

17. Add 1 to 2 tablespoons of the chicken filling in a line down the center and 1 tablespoon of cheese in a line alongside the chicken, leaving some space, ¼ to ½ inch, at the edges.

18. Bring the sides of the husk together over the filling. Fold the pointy tip of the husk over the filled section and secure the loose edge and pointy tip with a ¼-inch strip of husk tied in a knot. Set aside.

19. Repeat Steps 16 through 18 with the remaining masa, fillings, and husks.

20. To a large, lidded pot with a steamer insert, add the steamer insert and enough water to reach the bottom of the insert, about 2 inches. Place the pot over medium-high heat.

CONTINUES $\longrightarrow$

• Some grocery stores carry *masa preparada* (ready-made tamal dough). It typically comes plain, from nixtamalized white corn, but making it yourself allows you to add lots of flavor and spice.

• When you whip the lard or shortening, it will form peaks just like frosting or meringue.

• Don't submerge the tamales in the steaming water.

TIPS

• Corn husks sometimes have tears or deformities, so buy extra, just in case. If you want to make your own chicken, buy boneless and skinless and cook according to your preferred method.

• To test whether your masa is ready for cooking, fill a cup with water and drop 1 rounded tablespoon of the dough into it. If the dough floats, the masa is ready. If it sinks, the dough needs more liquid or fat.

21. Crumple a large sheet of foil to form a 3-inch-diameter ball, which will help the tamales stand upright. Place the ball in the center of the steamer insert and lean the tamales against it, open ends up and seam sides out.

22. Bring the water to a boil, then lower the heat to medium-low. Cover and steam the tamales until the dough firms, 40 to 45 minutes, adding more water if the level drops too low.

23. To check for doneness, remove a tamal from the pot and let it cool enough to handle. Try unwrapping it. If the dough sticks to the wrapper or foil, rewrap it, return it to the pot, and steam for 5 more minutes before checking again.

24. When the tamales have cooked, remove them from the pot and let them cool for 5 to 10 minutes.

25. Unwrap and plate them and drizzle with more salsa verde.

VARIATION

If you can't find corn husks, use 9-inch squares of foil instead.

Arkansas Delta Tamales

A tamal served with crackers and hot sauce? You bet. That's an Arkansas Delta tamal, also called a red hot. Tamales may have come to the Delta region, along the Mississippi River, in a few ways. In the late 1840s, soldiers from Arkansas fought in the Mexican-American War and may have brought a version of the dish back home, and Mexican migrants harvested cotton in Arkansas in the 1900s. However the dish arrived, it tastes great. Traditionally, the dough for these tamales consists of cornmeal rather than masa harina, but people today use both, and early versions used pork as the filling, but you can use beef or even turkey instead.

YIELDS 20 TO 25 SMALL TAMALES

Prep Time: 30 MINUTES
Cook Time: 3 HOURS
Total Time: 3 HOURS 30 MINUTES

FILLING

2 pounds pork roast
¼ cup vegetable oil
1 or 2 bay leaves
1 tablespoon chili powder
2 teaspoons ground cumin
1 teaspoon paprika
1 teaspoon freshly ground black pepper
1 teaspoon salt
½ teaspoon garlic powder
½ teaspoon onion powder
1 pinch cayenne pepper

DOUGH

2 cups lard or vegetable shortening
3½ cups reserved pork broth
2 tablespoons baking powder
2 tablespoons Sazón (page 197)
1 tablespoon salt
4 cups yellow cornmeal

Louisiana Hot Sauce (page 225) for serving

1. Make the pork: Bring a kettle of water to a boil.

2. While the water heats, rinse 27 corn husks in cold water to remove any debris.

3. In a large heatproof bowl, cover the rinsed husks with the boiling water.

4. Carefully place a heavy plate or other heatproof object on the husks to submerge them completely. Soak for 30 minutes.

5. Meanwhile, start making the filling: Cut the pork into ½-inch cubes.

6. In a large Dutch oven or heavy, lidded pot over medium-high heat, heat 2 tablespoons of the oil and cook the pork until it browns on all sides, 7 to 10 minutes.

7. Cover the pork with water and bring to a boil.

8. Add the bay leaves, cover, lower the heat to medium-low, and simmer until the pork becomes tender, 1 to 2 hours.

9. Remove the pork from the heat and reserve 3½ cups of the broth for the dough. Discard the bay leaves and any skin or large chunks of fat. When the pork has cooled enough to handle, use your fingers, 2 forks, or a stand mixer fitted with a paddle attachment to shred it.

10. In a large, heavy pot over medium heat, combine the remaining 2 tablespoons of vegetable oil, chili powder, cumin, paprika, black pepper, salt, garlic powder, onion powder, and cayenne.

CONTINUES ⟶

11. Add the shredded pork and coat evenly with the oil and spices. Cook, stirring often, until the pork heats through, 7 to 10 minutes. Set aside.

12. Meanwhile, start making the dough: Place the lard in the bowl of a stand mixer fitted with the whisk attachment. Whip the lard on medium-high until fluffy peaks form, about 20 minutes. The color will change from yellow to white.

13. Meanwhile, make the broth: In another medium bowl, whisk together the reserved pork broth, baking powder, sazón, and salt.

14. Working in batches of about ¼ cup, slowly pour the broth mixture into the whipped lard and whip at low to medium until the broth incorporates into the fat. Wait until each batch of broth incorporates completely before adding more liquid. Mix for about 5 minutes.

15. When all the broth has incorporated, switch out the whisk for the flat beater attachment. Add the cornmeal, 1 cup at a time, and beat on medium-high until the dough becomes smooth, 15 to 20 minutes. Set aside.

16. Meanwhile, drain the husks and shake off any excess water.

17. Tear 2 husks lengthwise, with the grain, into ¼-inch-thick strips. Set aside.

18. To the center of a husk, add about 2 tablespoons of dough (masa).

19. Using the back of a spoon, a soft spatula, or a masa spreader, spread the masa toward the widest part of the husk, leaving a small border, ¼ to ½ inch, all around.

20. Add 1 to 2 tablespoons of the filling in a line down the center of the masa, leaving some space, ¼ to ½ inch, at the edges.

21. Bring the sides of the husk together over the filling. Fold the pointy tip of the husk over the filled section and secure the loose edge and pointy tip with a ¼-inch strip of husk tied in a knot. Set aside.

22. Repeat Steps 18 through 21 with the remaining masa, filling, and husks.

23. To a large lidded pot with a steamer insert and a lid, add the steamer insert and enough water to reach the bottom of the insert, about 2 inches. Place over medium-high heat.

• When you whip the lard or
shortening, it will form peaks just like
frosting or meringue.
• Don't submerge the tamales in the
steaming water.

TIP

Corn husks sometimes have tears or
deformities, so buy extra, just in case.

24. Crumple a large sheet of foil to form a 3-inch-diameter ball, which
will help the tamales stand upright. Place the ball in the center of
the steamer insert and lean the tamales against it, open ends up and
seam sides out.

25. Bring the water to a boil, then lower the heat to medium-low. Cover
and steam the tamales until the dough firms, 40 to 45 minutes. Add
more water if the level drops too low.

26. To check for doneness, remove a tamal from the pot and let it cool
enough to handle. Try unwrapping it. If the dough sticks to the
wrapper or foil, rewrap it, return it to the pot, and steam for 5 more
minutes before checking again.

27. When the tamales have cooked, remove them from the pot and let
them cool for 5 to 10 minutes.

28. Unwrap and plate them and serve with soda crackers and hot sauce.

VARIATION

If you can't find corn husks, use 9-inch squares of foil instead. You also can use
masa harina for the dough and chuck roast or roast turkey for the filling.

Skirt Steak Fajitas

In Spanish, *fajita* means "belt" or "little strip," and this Tex-Mex dish—strips of skirt steak cooked by vaqueros on a campfire, *al carbón*—originated on cattle ranches in southwest Texas in the 1930s. But 1969 was the year of the fajita in the Rio Grande Valley. That year, Otília Garza bought the Round-Up Restaurant in Pharr and gave it to her regulars. It proved so popular that she quickly started selling it. Garza receives credit for the characteristic sizzling plate, which took inspiration from *queso flameado* (molten cheese) served on a cast-iron comal and the accompanying buffet of condiments. Also in 1969, Sonny Falcón ran the first fajita stand at a Mexican independence festival in Kyle. He later started the Fajita King chain but left the business in the 1980s, just as the fast-food mega chains, including Jack in the Box, were popularizing fajitas nationwide. Skirt steak was the original cut because it was cheap, but the law of supply and demand has changed the equation. Fajitas differ from tacos by being served on a sizzling skillet with grilled peppers and onions, tortillas on the side, whereas tacos consist of lots of different fillings served inside a tortilla, soft or hard. From this dish, many regional variations have emerged: Mexican fajitas, California fajitas, and more. Try them all but start with the original.

SERVES 4 TO 6
Prep Time: 4 HOURS
Cook Time: 20 MINUTES
Total Time: 4 HOURS 20 MINUTES

2 to 3 limes
½ green bell pepper
½ red bell pepper
2 cloves garlic
½ medium yellow onion
½ cup olive oil
2 tablespoons soy sauce
2 tablespoons Worcestershire sauce
1 teaspoon Adobo (page 196)
½ teaspoon ancho chile powder
½ teaspoon ground cumin
1½ pounds outside-cut skirt steak
2 tablespoons canola oil
8 to 12 Flour Tortillas (page 215)
Guacamole of choice (pages 200–203),
    Pico de Gallo (page 199), sour cream,
    shredded iceberg lettuce, pickled
    Jalapeño peppers, and chopped
    fresh cilantro for serving

1. Juice the limes. Stem and seed the bell peppers and slice them into ½-inch strips. Mince the garlic and cut the onion into ¼-inch slices.

2. In a large bowl, whisk together the olive oil, lime juice, soy sauce, Worcestershire sauce, adobo, chile powder, cumin, and garlic. Reserve ¼ cup of the marinade for later use.

3. Cut the steak into 3 equal pieces and place them in a large resealable plastic storage bag. Pour the marinade into the bag, seal, and massage the steaks for 2 to 3 minutes.

4. Marinate in the refrigerator for at least 30 minutes but ideally 4 hours.

5. When ready to make the fajitas, heat the oil in a large skillet over medium-high heat, then cook the onion, stirring, until softened, 4 to 5 minutes.

6. Add the bell peppers and cook, stirring, until softened, about 3 minutes. Set aside.

CONTINUES →

7. When the steaks have finished marinating, light a grill, heat a grill pan, or place a large skillet over medium-high heat. Place the steaks on the cooking vessel and grill, turning once, until medium rare, about 4 minutes total.

8. If using a grill pan or skillet, add the reserved marinade for some sizzle, 30 seconds per side.

9. Transfer the meat to a cutting board and let it rest for 3 minutes.

10. Thinly slice the steaks across the grain and plate on a serving platter with the cooked veggies.

11. Wrap the tortillas in a clean kitchen towel and heat them in a microwave on medium in 30-second bursts until warm, then plate with the meat and vegetables.

12. Serve with guacamole, pico de gallo, sour cream, shredded iceberg lettuce, pickled Jalapeño peppers, and chopped fresh cilantro.

VARIATION

If, where you shop, flank steak is less expensive than skirt steak, buy and use that instead.

Feijão Tropeiro

This traditional dish from Minas Gerais State originated among the *tropeiros* (cattle drivers) of Brazil in the 1600s. *Feijão* means "bean" in Portuguese, and this hearty stew combines Indigenous, Portuguese, and African influences. Crisscrossing Brazil's interior, tropeiros drove cattle and transported goods. Much like the chili bricks used to create Texas chili con carne in the 1850s (page 91), tropeiros created this field meal of dried beans, salted meat, and manioc flour while traveling. Today, the dish also typically includes onion, garlic, and collard greens or kale, and some Brasileiros like it with some crunch achieved by adding crumbled *torresmos* (pork rinds) on top. All of which aligns this stew with traditional American southern cuisine: beans, sausage, collard greens, and pork rinds. Sound familiar? Instead of *linguiça calabresa*, a Latino southern variation uses hot links or Louisiana red hot sausages. Chorizo or smoky kielbasa works, too. Brazilians eat it with fried (or sometimes hard-boiled) eggs for dinner, which, if you prefer, also makes for a robust breakfast or brunch.

SERVES 4
Prep Time: 14 HOURS
Cook Time: 2 HOURS
Total Time: 16 HOURS

1 pound dried carioca or pinto beans
2 bay leaves
8 ounces bacon
1 pound linguiça calabresa sausage
2 cloves garlic
1 medium yellow onion
2 tablespoons olive oil
1 bunch collard greens
4 large eggs
1 cup manioc (cassava) flour
1 teaspoon salt
Pork rinds for garnish (optional)
Green onions for garnish (optional)
Fresh parsley for garnish (optional)
Pão de Queijo (page 219) or Cilantro Lime Rice (page 209) for serving

1. Sort and rinse the beans.

2. In a large pot with a lid, cover the beans with water and soak, covered, for 12 to 14 hours.

3. Drain the beans, return them to the pot, cover them with water by 2 inches, add the bay leaves, and bring to a boil over medium-high heat.

4. Lower the heat to low, cover, and simmer until the beans cook through and become fork-tender, not mushy, 2 to 2½ hours.

5. About 10 minutes before the beans finish simmering, dice the bacon.

6. In a large skillet over medium heat, fry the bacon until crispy, 2 minutes.

7. While the bacon fries, cut the sausage into ½-inch slices.

8. Transfer the cooked bacon to a paper towel–lined plate to drain and cool.

9. In the same skillet over medium-high heat, cook the sausage slices until browned, about 3 minutes.

10. While the sausages cook, mince the garlic and slice or dice the onion.

CONTINUES →

Always sort through beans to ensure
they don't include any pebbles or
small rocks.

VARIATIONS

• Many grocery stores and online
retailers carry manioc or cassava
flour. If you can't find it, substitute
tapioca starch or coarse cornmeal.

• A pound of dried pinto beans roughly
equals 2 pounds 5 ounces or 6½ cups
of cooked beans.

• In lieu of soaking and cooking dried
beans, you can use three 15-ounce
cans of beans.

11. Transfer the cooked sausages to the same plate as the bacon.

12. Add 1 tablespoon of the olive oil to the skillet and sauté the onion
    until translucent, about 3 minutes.

13. Add the garlic and beans and cook for 5 minutes, stirring occasion-
    ally so the garlic doesn't burn.

14. While the mixture cooks, chiffonade the collard greens.

15. In a medium skillet over medium-high heat, heat the remaining
    tablespoon of olive oil and fry the eggs, sunny-side up.

16. To the skillet with the garlic and beans, add in the bacon
    and sausage.

17. Add the manioc flour, ¼ cup at a time, stirring to coat the meat.

18. Stir in the collard greens and salt, then cook until the greens begin
    to wilt, 1 to 2 minutes.

19. Remove from the heat, divide the feijão tropeiro among four plates,
    and top each with a fried egg.

20. Garnish with crushed pork rinds, diced green onion, and/or diced
    parsley to taste.

21. Serve warm with pão de queijo or cilantro lime rice .

Desserts

Postres

Sobremesas

Guava Cream Cheese Pastelitos

In Cuba, you can find guava everywhere, and few foods taste more Cuban than these flaky *pastelitos de guayaba y queso.* The earliest forms of the littles pastries featured just guava jam, no cheese, but an island precedent did exist for the delicious duo. Cubanos ate guava with white cheese, such as *queso fresco* or *queso blanco de jicotea*, on crackers. Old-school versions of this pastry contained lard, but today's *pasteleros* use shortening or butter. From the Spanish-American War until the Communist Revolution in 1959, America's influence on Cuba helped shape this confection. In those 60 years, American products, including Philadelphia brand cream cheese, came to the island. Then, fleeing the Castro regime, many Cubans brought their pastry traditions to America, primarily Florida. A Miami baker reportedly added cream cheese to a traditional pastelito de guayaba to create this Cuban-American treat. Multilayered like croissant dough, it contains thick, sweet guava jam, and the cream cheese tempers the fruit's hint of tartness and acid to create a mild, balanced sweetness. Other Latin American cultures also pair guava and cream cheese—with Dominicans calling the combination *Romeo y Julieta*, and some Puerto Rican *quesitos* (cheese rolls) containing guava filling—but these pastries taste especially Cuban.

SERVES 9
Prep Time: 5 MINUTES
Cook Time: 15 MINUTES
Total Time: 20 MINUTES

2 sheets puff pastry dough, 9¾ by
    10½ inches, at room temperature
5 ounces guava paste
5 ounces cream cheese
1 large egg white
2 tablespoons granulated sugar

TIP
You can make these "ravioli" style, all at once. Don't score the dough but still use the same 3-by-3 grid for each sheet, leaving about 1 inch of space around the fillings. Brush the egg white wash around all the fillings. Top with the second sheet of puff pastry, then slice it into 9 equal squares. Seal and crimp, then proceed with Step 8.

1. Preheat the oven to 375°F.

2. On a smooth, flat surface, using a rolling pin, roll out each sheet of pastry dough into a square.

3. Using a pizza cutter or knife, slice each large square of dough into 9 squares (a grid of 3 across by 3 down), for 18 squares total.

4. Place ½ to 1 tablespoon each of guava paste and cream cheese in the center of 9 of the squares.

5. In a small bowl, beat the egg white until frothy.

6. Using a pastry brush, lightly coat the edges of each filled square with the beaten egg white.

7. Cover the filled squares with the remaining 9 squares of dough. Using a fork or your fingers, crimp the edges to seal.

8. With a sharp knife, lightly score the top of the raw pastries 3 times.

9. Lightly brush the tops of the pastries with the beaten egg white and sprinkle with the sugar.

10. Bake until golden, 10 to 15 minutes.

11. Remove from the oven and let cool for 5 minutes, then serve warm.

Sopapillas

The name for these little fried triangular pastries has a fascinating history. It starts with *suppa*, Medieval Latin for "soup," which became *supa*, "bread soaked in oil," in Mozarabic, the Romance language spoken in Iberia during the Muslim Conquest. Andalusian Arabic modified that to *sappápa* (transliterated), with *sopáypa* as the diminutive. It came into Spanish as *sopaipa*, which received its own diminutive, *sopaipilla*, meaning a small, deep-fried pastry served with honey. Then the triangles traveled to the New World, ranging from Argentina and Chile to Mexico and New Mexico, each region developing its own traditions and variations. In New Mexican cuisine, savory ingredients—beans, cheese, meat, peppers—often fill them, though not always, while in the Tex-Mex tradition, they're always dessert, often dusted with powdered sugar and honey.

YIELDS 24
Prep Time: 30 MINUTES
Cook Time: 25 MINUTES
Total Time: 55 MINUTES

3 cups all-purpose flour, plus more for dusting
2 teaspoons baking powder
1 teaspoon salt
¼ cup vegetable shortening or lard
1¼ cups warm milk
Vegetable oil for frying
Dulce de Leche (page 228) for serving

1. In a large bowl, stir together the flour, baking powder, and salt.
2. With a pastry cutter or your hands, cut in the shortening.
3. Add the milk and mix the dough quickly by hand or with a fork until a dough forms.
4. Onto a well-floured surface, turn out the dough.
5. Knead the dough 12 times, or until it becomes soft and no longer feels sticky.
6. With a clean kitchen towel or plastic wrap, cover the dough and let it rest for 10 to 15 minutes.
7. In a large skillet or a deep fryer set to 400°F, heat at least 2 inches of oil.
8. Halve the dough and cover one portion with the towel or plastic wrap while working with the other.
9. On a flat, floured surface, using a rolling pin, gently roll the working portion to ⅛-inch thick.
10. Using a pizza dough cutter or sharp knife, cut the dough into 5-inch squares, then diagonally into triangles. Reroll the scraps to make more triangles.

CONTINUES ⟶

Instead of forming the dough by hand, you can use a stand mixer. Using the flat beater or paddle attachment on low speed, mix all the dough ingredients until they incorporate well, 2 to 3 minutes. Switch to the dough hook and mix on low speed for 2 minutes. If the dough sticks to the sides of the bowl, turn off the machine and scrape the sides with a soft spatula. Continue to mix until the dough becomes smooth and elastic and all the ingredients combine without sticking to the sides, 3 to 8 more minutes. If using a stand mixer, skip Step 5.

11. Repeat with the other portion of the dough.

12. With a spider skimmer or slotted metal spoon, carefully lower 4 to 6 raw sopapillas into the hot oil. Submerge them in the oil. They will puff immediately. Fry for 2 minutes.

13. Flip the sopapillas to fry the other side until browned, about 2 more minutes.

14. Transfer to a paper towel–lined plate to drain and cool.

15. Serve warm with dulce de leche and powdered sugar.

TIPS

• If not serving immediately, keep the sopapillas warm in a 200°F oven for up to 1 hour.

• Refrigerate leftovers and reheat them in a 350°F oven for 10 to 15 minutes before serving.

VARIATIONS

• Make it vegetarian by using vegetable shortening. Make it vegan by using your plant milk of choice.

• Eat them New Mexican dessert style by tearing off a corner and pouring honey into the pastry.

Plantain Upside-Down Cake

Anything bananas can do, plantains can do better. The two look-alike fruits originated in Southeast Asia as hybrids of two wild species. Bananas in America are usually the soft, sweet, yellow kind from the Cavendish family that you always can eat raw when ripe; they taste smooth and creamy. Plantains, common throughout Latin America, come in a range of shades: green, yellow, or dark brown. Larger and tougher than bananas, they have a much thicker skin and can taste sweet or savory. Green plantains often go into savory preparations, while yellow ones find their way into sweeter dishes, such as this one. Ripe plantains still have a dry texture and need lots of heat and fat to break down their starches to make them palatable. When cooked, they smell sweet like bananas, but they taste more vegetal. You can transform plantains into chips, *maduros*, mofongo (page 223), *patacónes*, and so much more. In America, the first published recipes for upside-down cake, which used prunes, appeared in the *San Francisco Chronicle* and the *Pittsburgh Press* in 1923. This recipe stretches the already versatile culinary capabilities of the powerhouse plantain to something new—and much tastier than prunes!

SERVES 8
Prep Time: 5 MINUTES
Cook Time: 50 MINUTES, PLUS
   COOLING TIME
Total Time: 1 HOUR 30 MINUTES

GLAZE
Unsalted butter or cooking
   spray for pan
¼ cup unsalted butter
½ cup dark brown sugar
1 pinch salt

CAKE
2 to 3 large or 6 small ripe yellow
   plantains
1⅓ cups all-purpose flour
1 teaspoon baking powder
½ teaspoon baking soda
½ teaspoon ground cinnamon
¼ teaspoon kosher salt
½ cup unsalted butter, at
   room temperature
¾ cup granulated sugar
2 large eggs
½ cup sour cream or Greek yogurt
Sea salt

CONTINUES $\longrightarrow$

• Look for the yellowest plantains you can find, with spots like a leopard. If you can't find fresh ones, check the freezer section.

• When still in the pan, don't let the hot cake cool for more than 10 minutes. If you do, the caramel will harden and glue the cake to the pan. You also don't want the cake to cool to room temperature because, if it does, the plantains will toughen.

• The cake tastes best right away, but you can store it, wrapped tightly in plastic wrap, in the refrigerator for up to 3 days.

1. Make the glaze: Preheat the oven to 350°F and butter the bottom and sides of a 9-inch springform pan with unsalted butter or spray it with nonstick cooking spray.

2. To help prevent leaks, wrap the outside of the pan with aluminum foil.

3. In a saucepan over medium heat, bring the butter and sugar to a boil. Stir, still boiling, until the sugar fully dissolves into caramel, 2 to 3 minutes.

4. Remove from the heat and stir in the salt.

5. Into the prepared springform pan, pour the caramel and, with a soft spatula, spread it evenly across the base. Work quickly and carefully before it cools.

6. Make the cake: Slice the plantains into halves or thirds lengthwise and arrange the pieces, cut side down, on the caramel, to cover it in a single layer.

7. In a small bowl, stir together the flour, baking powder, baking soda, cinnamon, and kosher salt. Set aside.

8. Using an electric whisk or a stand mixer fitted with the paddle attachment, cream the butter and sugar on medium speed for 1 to 2 minutes.

9. Add the eggs, one at a time, scraping down the sides of the bowl in between.

10. On low speed, add half of the flour mixture and mix until just combined.

11. Add the sour cream, mixing until just combined.

12. Add the remaining flour mixture and mix until just combined.

13. Pour the batter in an even layer over the plantains.

14. On a rimmed baking sheet, place the filled pan and bake until a toothpick inserted into the center comes out clean, 35 to 45 minutes.

15. Remove from the oven and let the cake cool in the pan for 5 to 10 minutes.

16. Onto a serving platter, invert the springform pan and release the cake from the pan.

17. Let the cake cool for 10 to 15 more minutes, from hot to warm.

18. Sprinkle with sea salt and serve.

Guava Cream Cheese Doughnuts

These doughnuts sold out. Let me explain. A famous New York City doughnut chain collaborated with me in 2021 and sold these handheld, heavenly confections. The doughnuts sold out every day, at every shop. We scheduled the collab for only one season, but these little stars accumulated fans. The chain occasionally brought them back into rotation, spurring a frenzy every time. Folks cried out for the chain to add my doughnut to the full-time roster. That didn't happen, so here's the recipe. The inspiration for it came from two sources. The first is my abiding love for jelly + carbs. I love a jelly doughnut, and I love that the first known recipe for one comes from the *Kuchenmeysterey* ("cake mastery") cookbook, created in Nuremberg in 1485, seven years before Columbus landed in the Caribbean. I also love jelly cookies and jelly on toast, and every Hanukkah, I buy *sufganiyot*. The second source of inspiration is my passion for adding guava and cream cheese to anything possible. Fried brioche encasing a rich balance of tropical sweetness and tartness—what more could you want?

YIELDS 8 DOUGHNUTS
Prep Time: 1 HOUR 30 MINUTES
Cook Time: 10 MINUTES
Total Time: 2 HOURS

DOUGHNUTS
One ¼-ounce packet active dry yeast (2¼ teaspoons)
¼ cup granulated sugar
½ cup warm water
2 large eggs
¾ cup warm whole milk (110°F)
½ cup unsalted butter, melted
½ teaspoon salt
4½ cups all-purpose flour, plus more for dusting
Canola or vegetable oil for bowl and pan
1 cup guava jelly or paste

FROSTING
8 ounces cream cheese, at room temperature
¼ cup salted butter, at room temperature
2 cups powdered sugar
1 to 2 tablespoons whole milk (optional)
½ teaspoon vanilla extract
⅛ teaspoon salt

1. Make the doughnuts: In the bowl of a stand mixer, stir together the yeast, 1 teaspoon of the sugar, and the warm water. Let stand for 5 minutes until the mixture activates, becoming frothy and bubbly.

2. While the yeast activates, lightly beat the eggs in a small bowl.

3. To the yeast mixture, add the remaining 3⅔ tablespoons of sugar, milk, butter, eggs, and salt.

4. Place the bowl on the stand of the mixer fitted with the dough hook and set to low speed. Gradually add the flour, 1 cup at a time, while the hook is spinning. Scrape down the sides occasionally until the dough gathers in the center of the bowl and becomes shaggy.

5. On a lightly floured surface, knead the dough until it becomes smooth and elastic.

6. Shape the dough into a ball, place it in a lightly oiled large bowl, and cover it with a clean, damp towel. Let rise at room temperature until it doubles in size, about 1 hour.

7. Meanwhile, cut parchment paper into sixteen 4-inch squares and arrange them in a single layer on 2 baking sheets.

CONTINUES →

8. When the dough finishes rising, remove it from the bowl, gently punch it down to deflate it, and halve it.

9. On a lightly floured surface, use a rolling pin to roll out half of the dough into a rectangle about 10 by 13 inches and ¼ to ½ inch thick.

10. Using a 3-inch-diameter cookie cutter or glass, cut out 8 disks, rerolling the scraps. Place each disk on a parchment paper square.

11. Repeat Steps 9 and 10 with the other half of the dough.

12. In a heavy skillet or deep fryer set to 375°F, heat 2 to 3 inches of oil. Check the temperature with a candy thermometer.

13. With a spider skimmer or slotted metal spoon, gently lower the doughnuts, 4 at a time, into the oil. Cook until golden, 2 to 3 minutes.

14. Flip the doughnuts and cook for 1 more minute on the other side.

15. Transfer the doughnuts to a paper towel–lined plate or wire rack over a paper towel to drain and cool.

16. Repeat Steps 13 through 15 to fry the remaining doughnuts.

17. Using a straw, skewer (preferred), or knife, cut a small slit, about ¼ to ⅓ inch wide, into the side and center of each doughnut.

18. With the guava jelly or prepared guava paste (see tips, below), fill a jam syringe, piping bag, or plastic storage bag with a corner snipped off.

19. Pipe approximately 1 tablespoon of guava jelly or paste into each doughnut.

20. Now, make the frosting: In the bowl of a stand mixer fitted with a paddle attachment, beat the cream cheese on high speed until smooth, 1 to 2 minutes.

21. Add the butter and continue to beat until smooth and well combined.

22. Gradually add the powdered sugar, milk (if using), vanilla, and salt and beat until smooth and combined. If the frosting is too thick, add 1 tablespoon of milk at a time until it reaches the right consistency.

23. With a knife or frosting spatula, frost the doughnuts and serve.

TIPS

To pipe guava paste, follow one of the following methods:

Food processor and microwave: Cut the paste into chunks and place in a food processor. Add 2 tablespoons of hot water and process for 20 seconds. Add 2 more tablespoons of hot water and process again until smooth. If the paste still looks chunky or isn't smooth and spreadable, add 1 more tablespoon of hot water and process. Transfer the paste to a microwave-safe bowl and microwave on high in 30-second increments, stirring between heating, until it becomes totally smooth. Let it cool enough to handle, 3 to 5 minutes, and proceed with piping.

Stovetop: Cut the paste into chunks and place in a medium saucepan over medium heat. Add 2 tablespoons of water. Melt the paste until smooth and pliable, stirring constantly with a wooden spoon or soft spatula so it doesn't scorch, 5 to 7 minutes. When picked up with a spoon, it should fall into ribbons. As it cools, it will firm and thicken. Let cool for 5 minutes and proceed with piping.

During frying, keep the oil between 310° and 350°F, which may require lowering the heat. Otherwise, the outsides will fry too fast, leaving the centers raw.

Fried Ice Cream

I know, it sounded over the top to me, too, at first. Why take ice cream, simply wonderful as it is, coat it, and *fry* it? But a moment of reflection changed my mind. Everyone has a favorite flavor, favorite toppings, a favorite way of eating ice cream, right? I'm a maximalist—the more mixings and toppings, the better—and the crunchy texture of "Mexican" fried ice cream certainly qualifies as maximal. The dish reportedly originated in the 1800s in Asia, and it came to Mexico with Chinese immigrants. In Mexico, it's called *nieve frita* (fried snow), and it uses a tempura-like batter: crushed corn flakes, other cereal, and sometimes whole slices of bread. In 1893, the ice cream sundae debuted at the Chicago World's Fair, and some accounts say that fried ice cream did, too, though we have no solid proof. The next year, the *Chicago Tribune* did run a story about a Philadelphia company inventing "fried cream," however. In 1975, restaurateur Marno McDermott—who had founded Zapata, a Mexican fast-food chain—and ex-footballer Max McGee founded Chi-Chi's, a Mexican restaurant named after McDermott's wife, in Minnesota. Chi-Chi's became a chain and popularized this hot-cold dessert nationwide before going extinct in North America in 2004. This recipe serves the dish "restaurant" style, on a fried flour tortilla sprinkled with cinnamon sugar, just as they did at Chi-Chi's.

SERVES 2

Prep Time: 2 HOURS 15 MINUTES
Cook Time: 1 MINUTE
Total Time: 2 HOURS 15 MINUTES

½ cup cornflakes

2 tablespoons granulated sugar

½ teaspoon ground Mexican cinnamon

2 large scoops French vanilla ice cream

6½ cups vegetable oil

Two 6-inch Flour Tortillas (page 215)

Aerosol whipped cream for garnish

2 maraschino cherries, with stems,
    for garnish

1. In a resealable plastic storage bag, place the cornflakes, seal the bag, and crush them with a rolling pin to the consistency of fine sand.

2. In a small bowl, stir together the sugar and cinnamon, then halve it.

3. Add the crushed cornflakes to one portion of the cinnamon sugar, stir to combine, and transfer to a wide, shallow pan, bowl, or plate.

4. Line a plate with parchment paper.

5. Place 1 large scoop of ice cream in the cornflake mixture.

6. With tongs, or your hands in food-grade gloves, roll the ice cream in the cornflake crumbs to coat completely.

7. Place the coated ice cream scoops on the parchment-lined plate and place in the freezer to harden again, 2 hours or longer.

8. In a medium skillet over medium-high heat, heat ½ cup of the oil and fry the tortillas, one at a time, until crispy and golden, 15 seconds on each side. Transfer to a paper towel–lined plate.

9. Sprinkle the remaining cinnamon sugar evenly over both sides of the fried tortillas and plate them.

10. In a large pot, Dutch oven, or deep fryer set to 350°F, heat the remaining 6 cups of oil.

• Alternatively, you can pulse the cornflakes to a powder in a food processor.

• An ice cream scoop with a trigger makes scooping easier, especially when making multiple servings.

• Before frying, the coated ice cream can keep in the freezer overnight. To keep longer, after the coated ice cream has firmed, place it in a resealable, airtight plastic storage bag or container.

11. Using a spider skimmer, lower the coated ice cream, one ball at a time, into the oil and fry for 2 seconds.

12. Place the fried ice cream in the center of a fried tortilla.

13. Spray whipped cream around the base of the ice cream and on top.

14. Top with a cherry and serve with honey and/or syrups of choice.

VARIATIONS

• Try Cinnamon Toast Crunch Churro cereal instead of cornflakes.

• If you don't have or don't want to use a deep fryer, roll the hardened ice cream balls in the cornflake and cinnamon sugar mixture and serve them atop the fried tortillas with all the fixings.

• To serve this dish "sherbet" style, as in the 1980s, squirt some whipped cream into the bottom of a serving glass. Place the fried ice cream on the whipped cream and drizzle a little honey over it. Place 8 whipped cream rosettes around the ice cream ball and one on top. Top with a maraschino cherry.

Guava Thumbprint Cookies

As a kid, newly arrived in America, making thumbprint cookies for the holidays felt like part of becoming a "real" American, as though baking cookies somehow led to citizenship. I did become a citizen but not from baking cookies or participating in Hallmark holiday traditions. As immigrants often do, I infused a local recipe with my own heritage, swapping out the raspberry or apricot jelly for guava paste. (See page 133 for more about the distinctly Cuban combination of guava and cream cheese.) In dessert form, these jewel-toned treats represent my assimilation into US culture while maintaining my "Cubanity" or Latinidad. A sweet testament to the holiday season and the power of combining cultures, they're as easy to make as they are delicious to eat.

YIELDS 36 TO 48 COOKIES
Prep Time: 2 HOURS 10 MINUTES
Cook Time: 40 MINUTES
Total Time: 2 HOURS 50 MINUTES

2¼ cups all-purpose flour
2 teaspoons cornstarch
1 teaspoon baking powder
¼ teaspoon kosher salt
½ pound (2 sticks) unsalted butter, at
   room temperature
⅔ cup granulated sugar
1 large egg
1 teaspoon vanilla extract
1 teaspoon almond extract
1 cup guava jelly or paste
Powdered sugar or coconut flakes
   for dusting

1. In a small bowl, stir together the flour, cornstarch, baking powder, and salt. Set aside.

2. In the bowl of a stand mixer fitted with the paddle attachment or a large bowl using an electric beater, beat the butter on low speed until soft, about 1 minute.

3. Add the sugar and beat until the mixture becomes fluffy, 3 to 5 minutes.

4. Add the egg, vanilla, and almond extract and continue to beat until the mixture combines well and becomes creamy, 1 to 2 minutes.

5. Add the flour mixture to the butter mixture and continue to beat until the dough comes together, 1 to 2 minutes.

6. Cover the dough and chill it in the refrigerator for at least 1 hour and up to 2 hours.

7. Preheat the oven to 350°F and line a baking sheet with parchment paper or a silicone baking mat.

8. Meanwhile, if using guava paste, use a wooden spoon to break the paste into chunks and melt the chunks in a small saucepan over medium heat until thick, smooth, and glossy, 10 to 15 minutes, stirring occasionally. Remove from the heat.

9. With your hands, roll 1 to 1½ tablespoons of the dough at a time into balls, arranging them 1 inch apart on the prepared baking sheet.

CONTINUES →

10. Using your thumb, press a cavity in the middle of each cookie. Don't press all the way through.

11. Spoon 1 teaspoon of guava paste into each cavity. It should form a slight mound.

12. Bake until the cookies barely turn golden, about 25 minutes.

13. Remove from the oven, transfer to a rack to cool, and sprinkle with powdered sugar.

NOTES

• Cornstarch makes the dough less sticky and allows the cookies to hold their shape.

• In an airtight container in the refrigerator, the cookies will stay fresh for up to 2 days.

Pavê

In 1874, Maria Romanova, daughter of Emperor Alexander II of Russia, married Alfred of Saxe-Coburg-Gotha, son of Queen Victoria of Britain, in St. Petersburg. Peek Freans, a London bakery, created the Marie biscuit in honor of the occasion. The couple's daughter Beatrice married into the Spanish royal family in 1909, and, after the Spanish Civil War in the 1930s, María cookies came to represent Spain's recovery. But countries all over the world make and enjoy the simple treat in a variety of ways, including with tea or custard and in cakes. In Brazil, *pavê*, a no-bake cake, consists of layers of brandy-soaked Marías and cream or custard. Some versions include fruit, chocolate, or coconut. According to food lore, the layers resemble cobblestones, and *pavê* means "paved." This cake is perfectly paired with Mojito Iced Coffee (page 188) or Mexican American Hot Chocolate (page 186).

SERVES 9 TO 12
Prep Time: 5 MINUTES
Cook Time: 5 MINUTES, PLUS
    CHILLING TIME
Total Time: 3 HOURS 10 MINUTES

CUSTARD

2 large egg yolks

**One 14-ounce sweetened
    condensed milk**

2 tablespoons cornstarch

1 cup whole milk

1 teaspoon vanilla extract

LAYERS

**4 ounces 100% cacao solid baking
    chocolate, plus more for garnish**

1 cup whole milk

1 to 2 tablespoons brandy of choice

36 María cookies

2 cups heavy cream

CHOCOLATE GANACHE

4 ounces dark chocolate

½ cup heavy cream

1. Make the custard: In a large pot over medium-high heat, whisk together the egg yolks, sweetened condensed milk, and cornstarch until smooth.

2. Whisk in the milk and vanilla and cook until the mixture simmers.

3. Lower the heat to low and cook until the custard thickens, 3 to 5 minutes. Remove from the heat and allow to cool.

4. While the custard cools, make the layers: Grate the 100% cacao chocolate and, in a small bowl, combine the milk and brandy.

5. One at a time, dunk 9 María cookies in the milk mixture for a few seconds each and, in a Bundt or 9-by-13-inch glass baking dish, arrange them in an even layer.

6. Pour one quarter of the custard over the cookies in the baking dish. Sprinkle evenly with 2 tablespoons of the grated chocolate.

7. Repeat Steps 5 and 6 three more times.

8. Whip the heavy cream on high speed in the bowl of a stand mixer fitted with the whisk attachment until soft peaks form, 7 to 8 minutes.

9. Spread the whipped cream on the pavê.

10. Refrigerate until the cake sets, about 3 hours.

11. About 30 minutes before serving, make the chocolate ganache: Rough chop the chocolate and place the chunks in a heatproof bowl.

CONTINUES ⟶

12. In a small saucepan over medium heat, heat the heavy cream until it simmers, about 5 minutes.

13. Pour the hot cream over the chopped chocolate and let it sit for 3 to 5 minutes to soften.

14. Whisk the chocolate cream until smooth.

15. Pour the hot chocolate over the cake. Use a soft spatula or tilt the baking dish so the chocolate covers the cake evenly and smoothly.

16. Refrigerate for 30 minutes.

17. Grate chocolate curls or crumbs atop the pavê to garnish and serve cold.

VARIATIONS

• If you like your desserts extra sweet, use solid dark or milk chocolate for the layers. If you want to go nuts, place ¾ cup of walnut pieces or nuts of choice in a small, dry skillet over medium-high heat. Toast the nuts in an even layer, stirring constantly so they don't scorch, for 5 minutes. Transfer them to a plate, spread them out, and let them cool for 5 minutes. Add them atop each custard layer.

• Instead of whipping the cream fresh, you can buy a 16-ounce tub of whipped cream, but don't use aerosol or canned.

• Instead of chocolate ganache topping, spread 2 cups of warmed Dulce de Leche (page 228) over the last layer of cake.

Dessert Tamales

If you like savory tamales, get ready to love their sweet siblings. The masa for these tamales differs slightly from the savory recipes, and masa harina, the instant corn flour in the dough, comes in a variety of colors: white, red, yellow, and blue. So have fun with these! Try matching the color of the corn flour to the color of the fruit filling(s). Use different individual colors to create rainbow tamales or mix 'em up for something a little more psychedelic. Think of the fillings as IHOP pancake toppings and check out the possibilities listed in the variations at the end of the recipe.

YIELDS 25 TO 30 SMALL TAMALES
Prep Time: 30 MINUTES
Cook Time: 3 HOURS
Total Time: 3 HOURS 30 MINUTES

DOUGH
1 cup vegetable shortening
4 cups masa harina (instant corn flour)
2 cups granulated sugar
2 teaspoons baking powder
1 teaspoon salt
2 cups milk of choice
1 tablespoon vanilla extract

FILLING
4 cups blueberries, fresh or frozen
¼ cup water
1 tablespoon fresh lemon juice
1 cup granulated sugar
1 pound cream cheese

Fresh whipped cream for serving

1. Bring a kettle of water to a boil.

2. While the water heats, rinse 30 cornhusks in cold water to remove any debris.

3. In a large heatproof bowl, cover the rinsed husks with boiling water.

4. Carefully place a heavy plate or other heatproof object on the husks to submerge them completely. Soak for 30 minutes.

5. While the husks soak, start making the dough: In the bowl of a stand mixer fitted with the whisk attachment, whip the shortening on medium-high speed until fluffy peaks form, about 20 minutes.

6. Meanwhile, prepare a blueberry compote for the filling: In a small saucepan over low heat, cook the blueberries, ¼ cup water, lemon juice, and sugar, stirring occasionally with a wooden spoon, until the blueberries start to burst, 10 to 15 minutes.

7. While the blueberries cook, continue to make the dough: In another large bowl, stir together the masa harina, sugar, baking powder, and salt.

8. After the shortening has whipped for 5 to 10 minutes, add the masa harina mixture to it.

9. Still while whipping, gradually add the milk and then the vanilla to the dough until it becomes creamy and airy, for the last 2 to 3 minutes of the 20 minutes for the shortening. This is your masa.

10. When the blueberries have cooked, remove the saucepan from the heat, and let the compote cool and thicken for 2 minutes. Set aside.

CONTINUES $\longrightarrow$

NOTES

• When you whip the shortening, it will form peaks just like frosting or meringue.

• Don't submerge the tamales in the steaming water.

TIP

These tamales also taste great for breakfast.

VARIATIONS

Experiment with different flavor combinations, such as chocolate, chili powder, and cinnamon; Dulce de Leche (page 228) and pecans; guava paste and cream cheese (of course); papaya or passion fruit and lemon curd; peanut butter and strawberry jam; and more. Incorporate your favorite fruits, nut butters, different kinds of chocolate, you name it. The world is your tamal!

11. In the bowl of a stand mixer fitted with the paddle attachment, beat the cream cheese on high speed until fluffy, 1 to 2 minutes.

12. Meanwhile, drain the husks and shake off any excess water.

13. Tear 2 husks lengthwise, with the grain, into ¼-inch-thick strips. Set aside.

14. To the center of a husk, add about ¼ cup of masa.

15. Using the back of a spoon, a soft spatula, or a masa spreader, spread the masa toward the widest part of the husk, leaving a small border, ¼ to ½ inch, all around.

16. In a line down the center of the dough, add 1 tablespoon of the compote and 1 tablespoon of whipped cream cheese.

17. Bring the sides of the husk together, over the filling. Fold the pointy tip of the husk over the filled section and secure the loose edge and pointy tip with a ¼-inch strip of husk tied in a knot. Set aside.

18. Repeat Steps 14 through 17 with the remaining masa, fillings, and husks.

19. To a large, lidded pot with a steamer insert, add the steamer insert and enough water to reach the bottom of the insert, about 2 inches. Place over medium-high heat.

20. Crumple a large sheet of foil to form a 3-inch-diameter ball, which will help the tamales stand upright. Place the ball in the center of the steamer insert and lean the tamales against it, open ends up and seam sides out.

21. Bring the water to a boil, then lower the heat to medium-low. Cover and steam the tamales until the dough firms, 40 to 45 minutes. Add more water if the level drops too low.

22. To check for doneness, remove a tamal from the pot and let it cool enough to handle. Try unwrapping it. If the dough sticks to the wrapper or foil, rewrap it, return it to the pot, and steam for 5 more minutes before checking again.

23. When the tamales have cooked, remove them from the pot and let them cool for 5 to 10 minutes.

24. Unwrap the tamales, plate them, and serve with freshly whipped cream.

Pumpkin Spice Tres Leches Cake

This recipe begins at the mall, in a Starbucks, while drinking an iced Pumpkin Spice Latte and eating a slice of pound cake. Cubans dip pretty much everything in coffee: bread, cake, cookies, even cigars. So I dunked a corner of the cake into the sweet, spicy beverage, and the result reminded me of a *cremosa pastel de tres leches* accented with warm baking spices. A uniquely American phenomenon, pumpkin spice has a surprisingly long lineage. Published in 1796, *American Cookery* by Amelia Simmons—the first cookbook written by an American—mentions it, and McCormick has been selling the spice blend since 1934. Starbucks released its Pumpkin Spice Latte in 2003, and it quickly became the company's most successful seasonal offering. But that drink sparked an unstoppable global trend that, for better or for worse, has affected nearly every food imaginable: beer, chips, cereal, hummus, Spam, vodka, yogurt, and more. If you can flavor it, someone already has pumpkin-spiced it. So, naturally, that's what I did, infusing it into a classic Hispanic dessert, pastel de tres leches. (See page 157 for more about Tres Leches Cake.) Pumpkin pie spices—allspice, cinnamon, cloves, ginger, and nutmeg—occur throughout Latin American cuisine in *antes* (fruit trifles), *buñuelos*, *cochinitos*, horchata (page 192), hot chocolate, moles, and more, but unlike many pumpkin-spice products, this dish contains pumpkin.

SERVES 14 TO 16

Prep Time: 10 MINUTES

Cook Time: 35 MINUTES, PLUS
    SOAKING TIME

Total Time: 8 HOURS 35 MINUTES

Cooking spray

2 cups all-purpose flour

2 tablespoons pumpkin pie spice

2 teaspoons baking powder

2 teaspoons baking soda

1 pinch salt

One 15-ounce can pure pumpkin puree
    (not pie filling)

¾ cup granulated sugar

¾ cup vegetable or canola oil

4 large eggs

1 teaspoon vanilla extract

One 14-ounce can sweetened
    condensed milk

One 12-ounce can evaporated milk

1 cup half-and-half

1½ cups heavy cream

1. Place a rack in the middle of the oven, preheat it to 350°F, and coat a 9-by-13-inch baking dish with nonstick cooking spray.

2. In a large bowl, combine the flour, 1 tablespoon of the pumpkin pie spice, the baking powder, baking soda, and salt.

3. In a medium bowl, whisk together the pumpkin puree, sugar, oil, eggs, and vanilla until smooth.

4. Add the pumpkin mixture to the flour mixture and stir thoroughly to combine.

5. Pour the batter into the prepared baking dish and, with a soft spatula, smooth it into an even layer.

6. Bake until a toothpick inserted in the center of the cake comes out clean, 30 to 35 minutes.

7. Remove the cake from the oven and, leaving it in the baking dish, let it cool enough to handle, 15 to 20 minutes.

CONTINUES $\longrightarrow$

NOTES

• Baked, cooled, covered, and stored at room temperature, the cake can stay fresh for 1 day before adding the tres leches.

• Don't overwhip the heavy cream or it will turn into butter.

• Covered in the refrigerator, the finished cake will stay fresh for up to 5 days.

TIP

You can buy pumpkin pie spice, but it's super easy to make your own with spices you probably already have in your cupboard or pantry: 4 teaspoons of ground cinnamon and ½ teaspoon each of ground allspice, cloves, ginger, and nutmeg.

8. With a hard spatula, loosen the edges of the cake, flip it over, and place it back, upside down, in the baking dish.

9. When the cake has cooled completely, use a fork or wooden skewer to poke holes all over the top, including the corners.

10. In a medium bowl, combine the three milks and slowly pour the mixture all over the cake.

11. Cover the dish with plastic wrap or aluminum foil and refrigerate for at least 3 hours or overnight.

12. When ready to serve, in the bowl of a stand mixer fitted with the whisk attachment, whip the heavy cream on high speed until soft peaks form, 7 to 8 minutes.

13. With a soft spatula or frosting spatula, spread the whipped cream on the cake.

14. Sift the remaining 1 tablespoon of pumpkin pie spice over the top, slice, and serve.

VARIATION

Instead of whipping the cream fresh, you can buy a 16-ounce tub of whipped cream, but don't use aerosol or canned.

Tres Leches Cake with Cream Cheese Frosting

This Latin American favorite follows the traditions of various European desserts—baba au rhum, bread pudding, fruitcake, rum cake, *sopa borracha*, tiramisu, trifle—but food historians generally trace its origins to Nicaragua in the 1800s. Dairy companies innovated canned milk in the 1850s, and the Managua elite ate a version of the dish called *delicias suecas* (Swedish delights). During the Great Depression, sales of affordable, shelf-stable dairy soared, and Borden, Nestlé, and other companies added this cake recipe to product labels to keep sales going. In 1936, America and Nicaragua signed a trade agreement that reduced import taxes on Wisconsin milk products, such as condensed, evaporated, and dried milk. In the 1970s, Nicaraguan cookbooks started including recipes for the dessert. But in 1972, an earthquake devastated Managua, and the Sandinista Revolution took place in 1979, both forcing thousands of Pinoleros to flee. Many settled in Miami's Sweetwater neighborhood, now called Little Managua, where Los Ranchos, a small Nicaraguan chain restaurant, opened in 1981, introducing the cake to the American market. As the dish was making its way to the United States, the rest of Latin America was falling in love with it, too, creating delectable variations, including chocolate, coconut, and versions with four, five, and even six milks. It has become a standard celebration cake for birthdays, family gatherings, and holidays. Despite being soaked, it doesn't taste the least bit soggy. Sweet and creamy, it has the texture of a custardy sponge cake and a luscious vanilla aroma.

SERVES 12

Prep Time: 25 MINUTES

Cook Time: 35 MINUTES, PLUS
    SOAKING TIME

Total Time: 9 HOURS

CAKE

Cooking spray

2 cups all-purpose flour

2 teaspoons baking powder

¼ teaspoon kosher salt

5 large eggs

1 cup granulated sugar

½ to ⅔ cup milk

1 teaspoon vanilla extract

3 tablespoons Grand Marnier (optional)

TRE LECHES

One 14-ounce can sweetened
    condensed milk

One 12-ounce can evaporated milk

1 cup half-and-half

FROSTING

8 ounces cream cheese, at room
    temperature

¼ cup plus 1 tablespoon
    powdered sugar

1½ cups heavy cream

2 teaspoons vanilla extract

12 maraschino cherries for garnish

Rainbow sprinkles for garnish (optional)

CONTINUES →

1. Make the cake: Preheat the oven to 350°F and spray a 9-by-13-inch baking pan with nonstick cooking spray.

2. In a medium bowl, sift together the flour, baking powder, and salt. Set aside.

3. Separate the egg whites and yolks.

4. In the bowl of a stand mixer fitted with the paddle attachment, beat the yolks and ¾ cup of sugar on high speed until the mixture turns pale yellow, 7 to 8 minutes.

5. Add the milk, vanilla, and Grand Marnier (if using) to the yolk mixture and mix on low speed until just combined.

6. Add the yolk mixture to the flour mixture and stir gently until just combined. Set aside.

7. Clean the bowl used for beating the yolk mixture. Add the egg whites and, using the whisk attachment, beat on high speed until they form stiff peaks, 5 to 10 minutes.

8. While beating the whites, slowly add the remaining ¼ cup of sugar.

9. Gently fold the egg whites into the batter until it just combines.

10. Pour the batter into the prepared baking dish and, with a soft spatula, smooth it into an even layer.

11. Bake until a toothpick inserted in the center of the cake comes out clean, 25 to 35 minutes. Remove from the oven and allow the cake to cool to room temperature.

12. When the cake has cooled completely, make the tres leches: In a medium bowl, combine the three milks.

13. Use a fork or wooden skewer to poke holes all over the top of the cake, including the corners.

14. Slowly pour the tres leches all over the cake.

15. Wrap the baking dish in foil and refrigerate for at least 2 hours or overnight.

16. While the cake soaks, make the frosting: In the bowl of a stand mixer fitted with the paddle attachment, beat the cream cheese, ¼ cup of the powdered sugar, the heavy cream, and vanilla on high speed until stiff peaks form, 7 to 8 minutes. Refrigerate until ready to serve.

CONTINUES ⟶

Fold the egg whites into the batter gently so the batter doesn't deflate.

17. Just before serving, let the frosting soften at room temperature for 5 minutes.

18. Use a soft spatula or frosting spatula to spread the frosting on the cake.

19. Dust with the remaining 1 tablespoon of powdered sugar.

20. Garnish with maraschino cherries and/or rainbow sprinkles, slice, and serve.

Stained-Glass Gelatin

Europeans have been making gelatin since the 1400s. After boiling animal tissue and bones, they strained, skimmed, and flavored the resulting thick mixture. Time-consuming and expensive, it evolved into a dessert that only the wealthy could afford. Colonists brought the tradition to the Americas. In 1845, Peter Cooper, who built the first American steam-powered locomotive, secured a patent for powdered gelatin. Some 50 years later, Pearle Wait added fruit flavoring and sugar to the mix, trademarking the result as "Jell-O." Since at least the 1940s, Mexicans have enjoyed gelatin treats in a variety of settings, from street carts to posh restaurants. In 1955, American home cook R. J. Gatti developed a version of this recipe, called Crown Jewel Dessert, and sent it to General Foods (now part of Kraft Heinz), the makers of Jell-O. The company popularized the dish by including it in cookbooks and other marketing materials. The American version includes pineapple juice, whipped cream, and a graham cracker crust. In Latin America, the dish contains only gelatin: milk-based white and fruit-based colors. The eye-catching dessert goes by several names, including broken glass cake and *gelatina de mosaico*, and it proves particularly popular in Mexico and Brazil. In Mexico, green lime, white milk, and red strawberry recreate the colors of the national flag. But how did Gatti come up with a recipe so close to the Latin American version? Chalk it up to different cultures having the same tasty idea.

SERVES 12

Prep Time: 30 MINUTES

Cook Time: 1 HOUR, PLUS
  CHILLING TIME

Total Time: 9 HOURS 30 MINUTES

Unflavored cooking spray

One 3-ounce box green gelatin

One 3-ounce box orange gelatin

One 3-ounce box red gelatin

3 cups hot water

One 14-ounce can sweetened
  condensed milk

One 12-ounce can evaporated milk

One 7.6-ounce can media crema, or 1
  cup whole milk

1 teaspoon vanilla extract

Four ¼-ounce packets
  unflavored gelatin

1 cup warm water

Fresh whipped cream and fresh fruit
  (optional) for serving

1. Lightly spray 3 small rectangular molds, such as plastic or glass storage containers, with unflavored nonstick cooking spray.

2. In 3 separate small bowls, fully dissolve 1 color of gelatin into 1 cup of hot water per bowl.

3. Add 1 cup of cold water to each bowl of hot gelatin and stir gently to combine.

4. Refrigerate the gelatins until firm and not sticky, at least 4 hours or overnight.

5. Cut the gelatins into ½- to 1-inch cubes.

6. In a blender, pulse the sweetened condensed milk, evaporated milk, media crema, and vanilla a few times to combine. Leave the milk mixture in the blender.

7. In a small bowl, combine all the unflavored gelatin and the warm water. Let sit for 5 minutes to thicken.

CONTINUES ⟶

8. Slowly add the thickened, unflavored gelatin to the blended milks and blend until homogenous, 10 to 15 seconds.

9. Spray a 6-cup Bundt pan or 9-by-13-inch baking dish with unflavored, nonstick cooking spray.

10. Working quickly in batches and mixing the colors, add a handful of the flavored gelatin cubes to the prepared pan, followed by 1 cup of the milk mixture. Repeat, alternating flavored cubes and milk mixture, until reaching ½ inch from the top of the pan.

11. Cover the pan with foil and refrigerate for 4 hours or overnight.

12. When ready to serve, gently release the sides of the pan by running a thin butter knife around the lip of the pan, no more than ¼ inch in.

13. Place a cake stand or serving platter upside-down over the pan, flip both, and slowly lift the pan to release the gelatin.

14. Slice with a sharp knife and serve with whipped cream and, if desired, fresh fruit.

Beverages

Bebidas

Oaxaca Old-Fashioned

The old-fashioned is the original cocktail. In 1806, Harry Croswell, editor of *The Balance and Columbian Repository*, published in Hudson, New York, defined a cocktail as "a stimulating liquor, composed of spirits of any kind, sugar, water, and bitters—it is vulgarly called *bittered sling*." When the Manhattan came along in the 1860s or '70s, vermouth revolutionized the drinking landscape, and the original cocktail became, well, old-fashioned. In Nahuatl, *mezcal* means "cooked agave," and Tequila, from the Nahuatl word *tequitl* meaning "the place of tribute," is a town in Jalisco State, around which blue agave grows plentifully. Oaxaca State produces 90 percent of Mexico's mezcal, and the International Mezcal Festival began there in 1997, several years before the cocktail renaissance started in New York City. In 2007, Phil Ward created this modern Mexican twist on the old-fashioned at Death & Co. in Manhattan's East Village. That bar—which I visited, one drink at a time, in my frugal 20s—later won the Tales of the Cocktail Best American Cocktail Bar and World's Best Cocktail Menu awards. My take on Ward's spec enhances the orange profile.

YIELDS 1 COCKTAIL
Prep Time: 2 MINUTES
Total Time: 2 MINUTES

1½ ounces Tequila reposado
½ ounce mezcal
½ ounce orange liqueur
¼ ounce agave nectar
2 dashes Angostura bitters
1 orange twist for garnish

1. In a mixing glass filled with ice, stir all the ingredients for 30 seconds.
2. Strain into a rocks glass filled with ice and garnish with the orange twist.

TIP
To elevate the drink, flame the orange peel. Strike a match or a lighter and carefully pass the outside part of the peel through the flame 3 to 5 times to activate the citrus oils. Rub the smoked peel around the rim of the glass and twist it, skin side down, over the drink before placing as garnish.

Texas Ranch Water

Summers in the Lone Star State often get too hot for heavy cocktails, so this thirst-quencher nicely fits the bill. As with many drinks, its definitive origins remain murky. One story credits it to Eloise Bryan at the White Buffalo Bar of the Gage Hotel in Marathon, Texas. Another contender, Kevin Williamson worked at the Gage and opened Ranch 616 in Austin in 1998 with Texas Ranch Water on the menu. The drink qualifies generically as a highball, which, borrowing from railroad terminology, originally indicated that you could make it quickly. Now, a highball means a base spirit mixed with a larger amount of an often-carbonated mixer. It also falls into the more specific rickey family of drinks—named for Joe Rickey, a southern lobbyist who made the original whiskey version famous in Washington, DC, in the 1880s—which contain lime juice and sparkling water. The simplicity of this cocktail offers lots of room for variations and customization. Some people add a little orange liqueur, agave syrup, or simple syrup for sweetness. You can spice the rim with chili-lime salt or Tajín (see Note on page 38) or, if you're feeling extra frisky, throw some Jalapeño slices in it. Just don't overdo it because the more you modify it, the more you dilute the magic of this straightforward, easy drink. It has become something of a cult classic, even appearing in cans, but fresh tastes best.

YIELDS 1 COCKTAIL
Prep Time: 2 MINUTES
Total Time: 2 MINUTES

Kosher salt for rimming

1 lime

2 ounces Tequila blanco

4 ounces Topo Chico sparkling mineral water

1. Rim a Collins glass with kosher salt, fill it with ice, and set aside.

2. Halve the lime and juice one of the halves for ½ ounce of juice. Cut the remaining half into wedges for garnish.

3. Add the Tequila and lime juice to the prepared glass and top with the sparkling mineral water.

4. Garnish with the lime wedges.

NOTE

When rimming a cocktail, sea salt is too coarse, and table salt is too fine. Onto a plate or shallow saucer, pour an even layer of kosher salt. Cut a small notch in the flesh of the citrus that corresponds to the cocktail (lime for cocktails containing lime, lemon for drinks with lemon, etc.), place the notch over the mouth of the glass, and rotate the citrus to coat the mouth with juice. Then twist the glass, upside down, in the salt. Always rim *before* adding ice.

Sparkling Caipirinha

In 1532, the Portuguese brought sugarcane from Madeira to Brazil. They fermented and distilled the raw cane juice into *aguardente de cana* ("fiery cane water"). Today known as *cachaça*—which, by law, only Brazil can produce under that name—it differs from rum in that rum typically ferments and distills from molasses, a by-product of refining sugarcane into sugar. Compared to rum's sweeter, vanilla notes, cachaça tastes earthy, musty, sometimes even sulfurous, but that doesn't stop Brasileiros worldwide from enjoying it in the country's national cocktail: the Caipirinha. In Portuguese, the word is the diminutive for a person from the Caipira people, in the south-central part of the country. (In the Indigenous Tupi language, *caipira* means "bush cutter.") Its definitive origins remain unclear, but spirits historians agree that it arose in São Paulo State around 1918. Today, many people drink Caipirinhas while eating *churrasco*, Brazilian steakhouse barbecue, and the popularity of the cocktail, following in the footsteps of the Margarita (page 170) and the mojito, is growing across America. The traditional recipe drinks *strong*, so I've softened it with some seltzer, which also adds a nice sparkle.

YIELDS 1 COCKTAIL
Prep Time: 2 MINUTES
Total Time: 2 MINUTES

1 lime
1 teaspoon granulated sugar
2 ounces *cachaça branca* or *prata* (unaged)
3 ounces seltzer

1. Quarter the lime into wedges.

2. In a rocks glass, gently muddle 3 wedges and the sugar.

3. Add ice and the cachaça and stir.

4. Top with seltzer and garnish with the remaining wedge.

NOTE
Don't use simple syrup or other liquid sweeteners in lieu of granulated sugar. When muddled, the sugar granules help extract oils from the lime peel.

VARIATION
For a classic Caipirinha, omit the seltzer and sip slowly.

Margarita

The daisy is an old family of cocktails made from a base spirit, citrus juice, and a modifier, usually a liqueur. Before Prohibition, the most popular drink in the family was the brandy daisy, and the sidecar cocktail is a Cognac daisy. *Margarita* means "daisy" in Spanish, the drink is a Tequila daisy, and it has many origin stories. Cocktail historian David Wondrich identified the first recorded instance of the drink in the *Moville Mail*, a small-town Iowa newspaper owned and edited by James Graham. In 1936, Graham and his wife took a trip to southern California and, while there, visited Tijuana. An Irishman named Madden ran a bar there, and he already had a reputation for inventing the Tequila daisy, which Graham described. The next year, the recipe appears in *The Café Royal Cocktail Book* by William Tarling, who calls it the Picador (a lancer on horseback in a Spanish bullfight). Perhaps Francisco Morales, a bartender at Tommy's Place bar in Juárez, Mexico, invented it in 1942. Whatever the origin, *Esquire* magazine published the first recipe for it by name in 1953. Jimmy Buffet's hit song "Margaritaville," released in 1977, made it even more popular, and in 2023, Nielsen, the media tracking company, confirmed that the margarita is America's most popular cocktail. Cheers to that!

YIELDS 1 COCKTAIL
Prep Time: 3 MINUTES
Total Time: 3 MINUTES

Kosher salt for rimming
½ lime
1½ ounces Tequila blanco
1 ounce triple sec
1 orange wedge for garnish

1. Rim a margarita or rocks glass with kosher salt and fill with ice.

2. Juice the lime half.

3. In a cocktail shaker filled with ice, combine the Tequila, triple sec, and lime juice and shake vigorously for 15 seconds.

4. Strain into the prepared glass and garnish with the orange wedge.

VARIATIONS

• The drink's proportions are as easy as 1-2-3: 1 part fresh citrus juice, 2 parts citrus liqueur, and 3 parts mezcal or Tequila. Use that template to experiment and build your own perfect version.

• You can serve it in a traditional margarita glass or, as pictured, a rocks glass.

• The traditional garnish is a lime, but this recipe switches it up for an orange wedge to highlight the drink's orange notes.

Daiquirí

In the 1700s, British sailors drank grog, a mixture of rum, lime juice, and water, named for Admiral Edward Vernon, called "Old Grog" for his grogram coat. In 1807, Frederic Tudor successfully delivered New England ice to Cuba, and a few decades later, Aeneas Coffey invented the column still in Dublin, which allowed for lighter, smoother spirits. In 1862, Facundo Bacardí y Massó pioneered a drier, lighter style of rum in Cuba using a column still, charcoal filtration, and oak barrels. The word *Daiquirí*, the name of a town on Cuba's southern coast, near Santiago de Cuba, comes from the language of the Taíno people, who lived on the island when the Spanish arrived. Many drink historians identify Jennings Cox, an American mining engineer working nearby, as the cocktail's inventor in 1898, just as the Cuban War of Independence exploded into the Spanish-American War. Writing to *El País*, Francesco Pagliuchi, a friend of Cox, described the drink as a shaken mix of Bacardi rum, lemon juice, sugar, and ice. Bacardí himself put Cox in the Venus Bar in Santiago de Cuba, which made the stirred drink with Bacardi rum, lime juice, and sugar over shaved ice. Either way, the drink is a Cuban-American classic.

YIELDS 1 COCKTAIL
Prep Time: 3 MINUTES
Total Time: 3 MINUTES

¾ lime
2 ounces white rum
¾ ounce Simple Syrup (recipe below)
1 lime wheel for garnish

1. Juice the lime.

2. In a cocktail shaker filled with ice, combine all ingredients and shake vigorously for 15 seconds.

3. Strain into a chilled coupe and garnish with the lime wheel.

NOTE

For simple syrup, heat ½ cup of water and ½ cup of granulated sugar in a small saucepan over medium heat, stirring until the sugar dissolves. Let cool to room temperature, transfer to an airtight jar, and refrigerate.

VARIATION

For a frozen Daiquirí, blend the ingredients with ¾ cup of ice until smooth. See page 173 for more about frozen Daiquirís.

Frozen Banana Daiquirí

If you think frozen Daiquirís aren't authentic, keep reading. Born in Barcelona, Constantino Ribalaigua i Vert came to Havana in 1900 as a young boy. He later joined the ranks of Bar la Florida, which he bought in 1918 and eventually renamed El Floridita. In 1924, he cofounded the Asociación de Cantineros de Cuba, the world's oldest bartender's society, and the next year he introduced an electric blender to his bar, allowing him to create the Daiquirí "en frappe." Some drink historians credit Harry Yee—who introduced paper umbrellas and edible orchids to mid-1900s cocktails—for adding a banana to the frozen Daiquirí in Hawaii.

YIELDS 1 COCKTAIL
Prep Time: 3 MINUTES
Total Time: 3 MINUTES

1 ripe banana
½ lime
2 ounces golden, spiced, dark, or black rum
1 ounce banana liqueur
½ teaspoon vanilla extract
½ to 1 cup ice

1. Peel the banana. Cut and reserve a slice from it for the garnish.

2. Juice the lime.

3. In a blender, blend the rest of the banana, the lime juice, rum, banana liqueur, vanilla, and desired amount of ice until smooth.

4. Pour into a hurricane or pint glass, garnish with the banana slice, and serve with a straw.

VARIATIONS

• Make it dirty by swapping out the banana liqueur for coffee liqueur.

• Have fun with the garnishes. Top with a dollop of whipped cream, a cocktail cherry, a drizzle of chocolate syrup, or a sprinkle of toasted coconut flakes.

Banana Daiquirí

Bananas originated in the islands of Southeast Asia and traveled along ancient trade routes and with the spread of Islam in the Middle Ages. In the 1500s, the Portuguese brought them to Brazil, and from there they proliferated in the tropical lands of the Western Hemisphere, including Cuba. Few activities feel more Cuban than eating bites of banana between savory mouthfuls, dipping cigars in coffee, or sipping a *carajillo* (coffee + rum) in the evening. This elegant cocktail combines the best of all worlds. A refreshing aperitif perfectly at ease with its flirty sophistication, it doesn't taste cloyingly sweet. Food lore credits its creation to the Mountain Top Bar in Saint Thomas, in the American Virgin Islands in the 1970s. The lime juice easily can overtake the subtle banana notes, so don't overdo it.

YIELDS 1 COCKTAIL
Prep Time: 3 MINUTES
Total Time: 3 MINUTES

¾ lime
1 ounce dark rum
1 ounce white rum
1 ounce banana liqueur
½ ounce Simple Syrup (page 172)
1 banana slice, with peel, for garnish
Juice the lime.

1. In a cocktail shaker filled with ice, combine all ingredients and shake vigorously for 15 seconds.

2. Strain into a chilled coupe and garnish with the banana slice, including its peel.

VARIATIONS

• Have fun with this one. Try starting with ½ ounce of lime juice.

• Play with different rums and even try adding bitters, which, like salt, can accentuate flavors. Angostura, orange, or even grapefruit bitters will work.

Tequila Sunrise

In the 1930s, Gene Sulit of the Arizona Biltmore Hotel in Phoenix combined Tequila, crème de cassis (blackcurrant liqueur), lime juice, and sparkling water to create the first version of this cocktail. In the 1970s, Bobby Lozoff and Billy Rice—bartenders at the Trident in Sausalito, across the Golden Gate Bridge from San Francisco—modified it to Tequila, orange juice, and grenadine. In 1972, Mick Jagger of the Rolling Stones tried it and loved it, and the next year the Eagles released a hit song by the same name, launching the sweet and tangy cocktail into one of the most iconic Tequila drinks in America. Go on, pour yourself a glass of daybreak.

YIELDS 1 COCKTAIL
Prep Time: 4 MINUTES
Total Time: 4 MINUTES

1½ oranges
2 ounces Tequila blanco
¼ ounce grenadine
1 orange wedge for garnish
1 cocktail cherry for garnish

1. Juice the oranges.

2. In a highball glass filled with ice, combine the Tequila and orange juice.

3. Add the grenadine, which will sink to the bottom, and garnish with the orange slice and a cherry.

Texas Margarita

So influential is Texas in the convergence of Latino and American cuisines that it has its own namesake margarita. (See page 170 for more about the margarita.) Like many beverages from the Lone Star State, it drinks easy and tastes sweet, refreshing, and citrusy. Everything's bigger, so it also contains additional ingredients.

YIELDS 1 COCKTAIL
Prep Time: 4 MINUTES
Total Time: 4 MINUTES

Kosher salt for rimming
¾ lime
⅓ orange
1½ ounces Tequila blanco
1 ounce orange liqueur
1½ teaspoons light agave syrup
1 lime slice for garnish
1 orange slice for garnish

1. Rim a margarita or rocks glass with kosher salt, fill with ice, and set aside.

2. Juice the lime and orange.

3. In a cocktail shaker filled with ice, combine the citrus juices, Tequila, orange liqueur, and agave syrup and shake vigorously for 15 seconds.

4. Strain into the prepared glass and garnish with the citrus slices.

The Siesta

In 1817, La Piña de Plata (The Silver Pineapple) opened in Havana, selling fresh juice. Over the decades, sales soared, the menu expanded, and in 1898 Narciso Sal i Parera, a Catalan immigrant, bought the venue and changed the name to Bar la Florida. Constantino Ribalaigua i Vert, another Catalan by birth, bought the location from Sal in 1918 and helped make it the "birthplace" of the Daiquirí. In the 1930s, Hemingway lived in and around Havana and spent a lot of time at La Florida. The story goes that he requested a Daiquirí with twice the rum and no sugar. Published in 1935, the *Bar la Florida Cocktails* guide includes that recipe as the "E. Henmiway Special," containing rum, maraschino liqueur, grapefruit juice, and lime juice. In 2003, Julie Reiner—later a winner of the Tales of the Cocktail Best Mentor and Lifetime Achievement Awards—opened Flatiron Lounge in Manhattan, which became an early epicenter of the craft cocktail renaissance. While working there a few years later, Katie Stipe created this showstopping drink by riffing on the Hemingway Special, swapping the rum for Tequila and substituting Campari for the maraschino.

YIELDS 1 COCKTAIL
Prep Time: 5 MINUTES
Total Time: 5 MINUTES

½ lime
1/12 grapefruit
2 ounces Tequila blanco
½ ounce Campari
½ ounce Simple Syrup (page 172)
1 citrus twist or slice for garnish

1. Juice the lime and grapefruit.

2. In a cocktail shaker filled with ice, combine the citrus juice, Tequila blanco, Campari, and simple syrup and shake vigorously for 15 seconds.

3. Strain into a chilled coupe and garnish with the citrus twist or slice.

Piña Colada

One of the golden rules of recipe development and food pairings is: What grows together goes together. Pineapples and sugarcane both grow in tropical climates, so combining rum and pineapple makes good sense. After the Spanish-American War—when Puerto Rico became an organized territory of America and Cuba came under US military control—travel to both islands boomed, and drinking *jugo de piña con ron* (pineapple juice with rum) became fashionable. *Piña colada* means "strained pineapple," and the first written reference to the cocktail (rum, pineapple, lime, sugar) occurs in a 1922 *Travel* magazine article about Havana. Harry Craddock included the drink in *The Savoy Cocktail Book*, published in 1930, and the Havana Beach cocktail in *Bar la Florida Cocktails*, published in 1935, contains rum, pineapple, and sugar. But what about the coconut cream? Historians largely agree that Ramón Marrero y Perez, a bartender at the Caribe Hilton Hotel in San Juan, Puerto Rico, created this distinctly Puerto Rican version there in 1954. Some argue that Ramón Portas y Mingot created it at the Barrachina Restaurant, also in San Juan, in 1963, but Puerto Rico named the drink its official cocktail in 1978, confirming Marrero as its creator.

YIELDS 1 COCKTAIL
Prep Time: 5 MINUTES
Total Time: 5 MINUTES

½ fresh pineapple (about 1 cup juice)
2 ounce white rum
2 ounces coconut cream
½ cup ice
Pineapple chunks for garnish

1. Juice the pineapple.

2. In a blender, blend the pineapple juice, rum, coconut cream, and ice until smooth.

3. Pour into a hurricane or pint glass, garnish with pineapple chunks, and serve with a straw (optional).

VARIATION

For a little more flair, top the finished drink with whipped cream and a cocktail cherry or two as additional garnish.

Frozen Mango Margarita

Americans like it cold: air-conditioning, ice water, iced coffee, coffee slushies, fruity slush-ies, frozen margaritas. In the early 1800s, Frederic Tudor made—and lost and remade—his fortune selling Massachusetts ice around the world, from Havana and Hong Kong to Madras and Martinique. He harvested it from his father's farm, insulated it with sawdust or rice chaff, and built icehouses for storage in destination markets, including Charleston, Savannah, New Orleans, and other southern American cities. Low temperatures dull our sense of taste, which may sound bad, but in practice that reduces the perception of excessive sweetness and bit-terness in alcoholic drinks. (That's also why beverage manufacturers often suggest drinking bottom-shelf products ice cold.) So it should come as no surprise that the margarita craze went slushy. In 1971, Mariano Martinez, a Dallas restaurateur, was trying to keep customers craving blender margs happy while also making the work easier for his kitchen staff. He tried to buy one of 7-Eleven's Slurpee machines, but the company wouldn't sell to him. Instead, he bought a secondhand ice cream machine, which he retrofitted for drinks. The frozen mar-garita machine helped popularize the drink even more. Martinez didn't patent his invention, but in 2005, when the original machine had run its course, the National Museum of American History in Washington, DC, happily accepted it into their permanent collection.

YIELDS 1 COCKTAIL
Prep Time: 5 MINUTES
Total Time: 5 MINUTES

Tajín for rimming (for homemade, see
    Note on page 38)
1 lime
1½ ounces fresh mango
1½ ounces Tequila blanco
1 ounces orange liqueur
½ cup ice

1. Rim a chilled coupe with Tajín, then set aside.

2. Juice three-quarters of the lime, reserving the remaining wedge.

3. In a blender, pulse the mango to break it apart, then puree.

4. Add the Tequila blanco, orange liqueur, and ice, then blend until smooth.

5. Pour into the prepared glass and garnish with the reserved lime wedge.

Mexican American Hot Chocolate

The origins of hot chocolate date back millennia to the Indigenous cultures of Central America, primarily in Mexico, where people consumed it neither hot nor sweet. As early as 500 BC, Mayans were drinking chocolate made from ground cocoa seeds mixed with water, cornmeal, and chile peppers. Modern Mexican hot chocolate also contains bittersweet chocolate for a rich but not-so-sweet beverage, and it features warming spices, such as cinnamon and chili powder. You may not know of Charles Sanna, but you probably know Swiss Miss, the iconic American brand of powdered hot chocolate mix. In the early 1950s, his company, Sanna Dairy Engineers (amazing), produced powdered creamer packets for American troops fighting in the Korean War, and the company found itself with a surplus. To use the extra powdered creamer, Sanna combined it with cocoa, sugar, and vanilla to create Swiss Miss, the first instant hot chocolate mix designed to be made with hot water instead of milk, though, as with oatmeal, milk makes it taste even better. For civilian purposes, Sanna sold it first to airlines. When it had proven itself, grocery stores ordered it. Later, he swapped the creamer for nonfat milk powder. This recipe combines the best of Mexican and American hot chocolates: The convenience of a creamy, premade powder meets rich, flavorful spices.

SERVES 5 TO 7
Prep Time: 5 MINUTES
Cook Time: 2 MINUTES
Total Time: 7 MINUTES

1½ cups whole milk powder

1 cup powdered sugar

¾ cup unsweetened cocoa powder

¾ cup white chocolate chips

2½ teaspoons ground cinnamon

1¼ teaspoons dried vanilla powder (optional)

1 teaspoon cornstarch

¾ teaspoon cayenne pepper, or more to taste

¾ teaspoon chili powder, or more to taste

⅛ teaspoon salt

Milk of choice

Whipped cream or marshmallows for garnish (optional)

1. In a food processor, pulse the milk powder, powdered sugar, cocoa powder, white chocolate chips, cinnamon, vanilla powder (if using), cornstarch, cayenne, and chili powder until the chocolate grinds to a fine powder. Store in an airtight container in a cool, dark place for up to 3 months.

2. When ready to serve, microwave 1 cup milk of choice on high for 2 minutes.

3. Into the hot milk, whisk ¼ to ⅓ cup of the cocoa mix until the mix dissolves completely.

4. Top with whipped cream or marshmallows, if desired.

TIP

Instead of a whisk, use a milk frother to dissolve the mix in the milk with minimal effort.

Mojito Iced Coffee

The ancient Greeks used mint as an air freshener and, more importantly for our purposes, to treat stomach ailments and discomfort, a Mediterranean tradition that the Spanish brought to the Western Hemisphere. Dispatched by Queen Elizabeth I of England to attack Spain's colonies in the New World, Sir Francis Drake embarked in 1585 on his Great Expedition, in which, among other mayhem, he planned to sack Havana, but his crew fell ill. His ships carried aguardiente, and many of the ports that he raided today feature drinks with names closely related to his Spanish nickname: El Draque (the dragon). In Venezuela, a *draque* contains aguardiente and serves as a stomach remedy. An energetic herbal tisane in Mexico, it aids with rehydration in Colombia. At La Concha beach bar in Marianao, Cuba, the draque morphed into a Ron Collins—rum, lemon juice, sugar, Angostura bitters, club soda—that the bar called a *mojito*, which means "little sauce or mixture" in Spanish. In the 1935 Bar la Florida cocktail guide, the Mojito Criollo drops the bitters and adds mint. In 1942 in Old Havana, Angel Martínez bought Bodega la Complaciente, renaming it Casa Martínez and serving mojitos as we know them today. (In 1950, Martínez changed the name again to Bodeguita del Medio.) As below, you can add dark rum, which plays well with coffee, to this caffeinated take on the mojito.

YIELDS 1 DRINK
Prep Time: 5 MINUTES
Cook Time: 5 MINUTES
Total Time: 10 MINUTES

1 lime

6 to 8 fresh leaves mint

2 tablespoons dark brown or turbinado sugar

2 shots freshly made espresso or 1 cup freshly made hot coffee of choice

1 sprig mint for garnish

1. Zest the entire lime.

2. In a bowl or large measuring cup, gently muddle the mint, brown sugar, and lime zest. Extract the mint oils but don't tear the leaves, which, if you do, will release bitter-tasting compounds.

3. Pour the freshly made espresso or coffee over the muddled mint mixture. Let steep for 3 minutes.

4. Transfer the mixture to a cocktail shaker filled with ice, then shake vigorously for 15 seconds.

5. Strain into a Collins glass filled with ice, garnish with the mint sprig.

VARIATIONS

• Instead of making hot coffee or espresso, you can use cold brew. In 12 ounces of cold brew, steep the mint leaves for 4 hours or overnight.

• To make a latte, add ½ cup of milk or plant milk or ¼ cup half-and-half or heavy cream to the shaker.

• To make it an adult beverage, add 1 ounce of dark rum or rum-based coffee liqueur or cream coffee liqueur, such as Kahlúa or RumChata, to the shaker. If using a liqueur, adjust the amounts of coffee and milk or cream to taste.

Tres Leches Latte

Tres Leches Cake (page 157), but make it coffee. The creamy sweetness of tres leches transforms a traditional latte in much the same way as Vietnamese iced coffee and Thai iced tea, which also use sweetened condensed milk.

SERVES 4

Prep Time: 5 MINUTES, PLUS CHILLING TIME

Total Time: 35 MINUTES

One 14-ounce can sweetened condensed milk

One 12-ounce can evaporated milk

1 cup half-and-half

½ teaspoon vanilla extract

Cold-brew coffee, espresso, or coffee of choice

1. In a small pitcher or bottle, combine the three milks and vanilla and refrigerate for 30 minutes.

2. When ready to serve, fill a Collins or pint glass with ice.

3. Add 1 to 2 ounces of coffee to the glass, followed by 8 ounces of the tres leches mixture.

4. Stir to combine and serve with a straw.

NOTE

A standard latte contains 1 or 2 ounces of espresso and 8 to 10 ounces of milk.

Tex-Mex Horchata

This sometimes-rice-based beverage originated in North Africa and has Arabic roots, spreading with Islam to Spain in the Middle Ages and then to the Western Hemisphere. The word comes from *hordeata*, Latin for "barley." Growing up, I drank ice-cold horchata made with rice, coconut milk, and a pinch of cinnamon, and in college I slapped together a buy-and-pour version with those ingredients. Latin American varieties tasted on my travels contain cow's milk, *jicaro* (calabash), melon, or sesame seeds. In Spain, beautifully tiled *horchaterías* serve the mother—*horchata de chufa*, made from tiger nuts—which I had the privilege of enjoying when living in Madrid and traveling the country. It drank much thicker than the style of my childhood. Mexican horchata contains rice and/or almonds, while the Texan adaptation skips the almonds and sometimes includes milk. You can find the horchata flavor profile in coffees, creamers, doughnuts, ice creams, and more, but make it yourself before you branch out. This Tex-Mex recipe drinks more like *agua fresca* than the creamy, thicker versions in Spain.

YIELDS 2 QUARTS
Prep Time: 5 MINUTES
Cook Time: 4 HOURS 10 MINUTES
Total Time: 4 HOURS 15 MINUTES

½ cup uncooked long-grain white rice
2 cinnamon sticks
½ to 1 cup granulated sugar
    or panela/rapadura
1 tablespoon vanilla extract

1. In a large lidded pot over high heat, bring 2 quarts of water to a boil.

2. While the water heats, rinse the rice.

3. Add the rinsed rice and cinnamon to the boiling water. Lower the heat to low and simmer until the rice becomes tender, 10 to 15 minutes.

4. Remove from the heat, cover, and steep for 2 to 3 hours.

5. Remove the cinnamon sticks and transfer the rice mixture to a blender. Blend until completely smooth.

6. Through a large, fine-mesh sieve or cheesecloth, pour the mixture into a large lidded pitcher.

7. Add the desired amount of sugar and the vanilla, stir to dissolve, and refrigerate for at least 2 hours.

8. Pour into Collins glasses filled with ice and serve with a straw.

VARIATIONS

• For even more aromatic flavor, add 5 to 7 whole cardamom pods along with the cinnamon sticks and remove before blending.

• Some folks add 1 teaspoon of fresh lime zest during the boiling process and serve the drink with a squeeze of fresh lime.

• For a creamier Texas horchata, add 12 to 14 ounces of your milk of choice, such as sweetened condensed milk, coconut milk, or almond milk.

Spices, Sauces, Sides, and Staples

Especias, Salsas, Acompañamientos, y Alimentos Básicos

Especiarias, Molhos, Acompanhamentos, e Alimentos Básicos

Adobo

Hailing from wet marinades in Spanish and Portuguese culinary traditions, this essential, all-purpose blend of spices occurs as frequently as salt and pepper throughout Latin American, Caribbean, and American Latino cuisines. The salty taste and garlicky flavor make it great for adding savory notes to beans, fish, meats, sauces, soups, stews, stock, and vegetables. Depending on the proportions of the various ingredients, it can run the gamut from pale, through yellow, to red. Some adobo blends contain turmeric or citrus, and it works great as a protein rub.

YIELDS ½ CUP
Prep Time: 2 MINUTES
Total Time: 2 MINUTES

2 teaspoons freshly ground black pepper
2 tablespoons salt
1½ teaspoons dried oregano
1 tablespoon garlic powder
1 tablespoon onion powder
1 tablespoon paprika
2 teaspoons ground cumin
1 teaspoon chili powder

1. In a small bowl, stir together all the ingredients.

2. Transfer to a sealable jar and store in a cool, dry place.

Sazón

This versatile, savory spice blend, its name meaning "seasoning" in Spanish, has many dimensions of flavor. The color ranges from yellow, through red, to brown. The yellow-orange tones come from achiote, a plant native to the tropical regions of the Americas, which yields annatto, a food coloring that tastes nutty and peppery. Use sazón in marinades. Sprinkle it on any dish that calls for savory seasoning. Rub it into your protein of choice: beef, chicken, fish, pork, or tofu. You'll want to put it on everything, and you should.

YIELDS ½ CUP
Prep Time: 3 MINUTES
Total Time: 3 MINUTES

2 tablespoons achiote seeds (annatto)

2 tablespoons salt

1 tablespoon coriander seeds

1 tablespoon cumin seeds

1 tablespoon garlic powder

1 tablespoon onion powder

1 teaspoon dried oregano

½ teaspoon freshly ground black pepper

1. In a small bowl, stir together all the ingredients.

2. Working in batches, transfer the spice mixture to a coffee/spice grinder, mortar and pestle, or molcajete (page 201) and grind to a powder. If desired, sift the powder through a fine-mesh sieve to filter out any large grains.

3. Transfer the sazón to an airtight container and store in a dry, dark place at room temperature.

NOTE
Properly stored, sazón will keep for up to 1 year.

VARIATIONS
• Adjust the proportions of the ingredients to taste.

• For smoky sazón, add 1½ teaspoons of smoked paprika to the mixture.

Taco Seasoning

Chili powder, invented in 1894 by German Texan William Gebhardt, made the success of the American hard-shell taco and its descendants possible, and chili powder constitutes the chief ingredient in taco seasoning. In 1938, brothers-in-law Lawrence Frank and Theodore van de Kamp opened Lawry's The Prime Rib restaurant in Beverly Hills, California, and the same year began selling their famous seasoned salt. They added taco seasoning to the mix in 1967. Perfect for seasoning beans, beef, chicken, and tofu, it adds a warm, earthy, savory taste to many dishes.

YIELDS APPROXIMATELY 3 TABLESPOONS

Prep Time: 3 MINUTES

Total Time: 3 MINUTES

1 tablespoon chili powder

1½ teaspoons ground cumin

1 teaspoon cornstarch

1 teaspoon freshly ground black pepper

1 teaspoon salt

½ teaspoon paprika

¼ teaspoon garlic powder

¼ teaspoon onion powder

¼ teaspoon dried Mexican oregano

In a small bowl, stir together all the ingredients.

NOTE

One store-bought packet of taco seasoning contains 2 tablespoons.

VARIATION

Taco seasoning with more of a fiery kick owes that heat to ancho chiles. Start with ¼ teaspoon of ancho chile powder and increase to taste.

Pico de Gallo

In his *General History of the Aspects of New Spain*, Bernardino de Sahagún describes what we call pico de gallo in a survey of food sold in Aztec markets, and Alonso de Molina, another Franciscan friar, later identified it as a salsa. (All pico de gallo is salsa, but not all salsa is pico de gallo. Pico de gallo contains fresh, raw ingredients, whereas salsa mostly consists of blended, cooked, or mashed ingredients.) In Spanish, the name means "rooster's beak." Explanations abound, but the most likely point to the Serrano pepper looking like a rooster's beak and *picar* in Spanish meaning "to have bite." It also goes by other names, including *salsa bandera* (for the colors of the Mexican flag), *salsa cruda* (raw), *salsa fresca* (fresh), and *salsa Mexicana*. Add it to anything that calls for a refreshing pop of crunch, tang, and zing.

YIELDS 2 TO 3 CUPS
Prep Time: 10 MINUTES
Total Time: 10 MINUTES

6 ripe Roma tomatoes
½ lime
2 cloves garlic
½ to 1 Jalapeño pepper
½ small to medium red onion
¼ cup chopped fresh cilantro
1 pinch ground cumin
1 pinch garlic powder
Salt and freshly ground black pepper

1. Dice the tomatoes, juice the ½ lime, mince the garlic, seed and mince the Jalapeño pepper, and mince the onion. Combine all in a medium bowl.

2. Add the cilantro, cumin, garlic powder, and salt and black pepper to taste.

3. Taste, adjust any ingredients to preference, and serve.

Mission Guacamole

Avocados originated in the southernmost reaches of North America, and, as with Pico de Gallo (page 199), we have records from the 1500s that describe people eating guacamole in the Aztec Empire. The Nahuatl word *ahuacamolli* means "avocado mixture (or sauce)." Mexican immigrants brought guacamole to America in the 1930s after many of them had escaped the violence of the Mexican Revolution (1910–1920). Around this time, an American ban on Mexican goods lifted, allowing avocados, then called alligator pears, to enter the market. But not until the North American Free Trade Agreement, which came into effect in 1994, did guacamole soar in popularity. My favorite guacamole comes from Chipotle, and I call it Mission Guacamole after the San Francisco neighborhood from which the chain took its inspiration when its first location opened in Denver. Chipotle's recipe remains a trade secret, but this one comes mighty close.

SERVES 4
Prep Time: 10 MINUTES
Total Time: 10 MINUTES

¼ teaspoon cumin seeds
2 large ripe Hass avocados
½ Jalapeño pepper
1 teaspoon fresh lemon juice
1 teaspoon fresh lime juice
¼ cup finely chopped red onion
2 tablespoons finely chopped fresh cilantro leaves
Salt

1. In a small skillet over medium-high heat, toast the cumin seeds until fragrant, occasionally shaking the skillet to prevent scorching, about 30 seconds.

2. Transfer the toasted seeds to a small dish and let them cool to room temperature.

3. While the cumin cools, halve and pit the avocados and, still in the peel, slice the flesh into chunks. Stem, seed, and finely chop the Jalapeño pepper.

4. In a medium bowl, mash the avocado chunks and citrus juices until smooth.

5. Add the red onion, cilantro, and Jalapeños.

6. When the cumin has cooled, grind it in a spice/coffee grinder, mortar and pestle, or molcajete (page 201) to a fine powder. Add to the guacamole and season with salt to taste.

7. Serve immediately or refrigerate to a light chill, about 5 minutes.

NOTE

Many of the recipes in this book call for freshly toasted and ground cumin seeds. Those two extra steps add a lot more body and flavor than pre-ground cumin. Trust me, it'll make your guac pop. If you can't or don't want to toast and grind it, store-bought is fine (said in my best Ina Garten voice).

American Guacamole

In 1912, the *New York Times* ran an article called "Avocado Pear Recipes" that included one for Aguncate Salad, a pounded mixture of avocados, tomatoes, green peppers, onion juice, and lemon juice or vinegar. *Fashions in Food in Beverly Hills*—a cookbook published by the Beverly Hills Women's Club in 1929 as a fundraiser—contains a "Wakimoli Salad," which includes mayonnaise and paprika and calls the main ingredient "calavos," a term that the California Avocado Growers Exchange had trademarked in 1926. Mexican guacamole runs a little thinner and doesn't include dairy, while chunkier American versions often contain sour cream or mayonnaise.

SERVES 4
Prep Time: 10 MINUTES
Total Time: 10 MINUTES

2 ripe Hass avocados

¼ cup sour cream or mayonnaise

1 teaspoon fresh lime juice

½ to 1 teaspoon Adobo (page 196)

2 tablespoons finely chopped cilantro leaves

Salsa Roja (page 217), Salsa Verde (page 226), Pico de Gallo (page 199), Louisiana Hot Sauce (page 225), or red pepper flakes for serving

1. Halve and pit the avocados and, still in the peel, slice the flesh into chunks.

2. In a small bowl or molcajete (page 201), mash the avocado chunks until very smooth.

3. Add the sour cream and lime juice and stir to combine.

4. Season with desired amount of adobo, stir again, and garnish with the chopped cilantro.

5. Serve immediately with salsa or pico de gallo, or a few shakes of hot sauce or red pepper flakes, or refrigerate to a light chill, about 5 minutes.

VARIATIONS

• Substitute Greek yogurt for the sour cream or mayonnaise.

• Instead of adobo, try Taco Seasoning (page 198) or ranch seasoning.

Herby Guacamole

Guacamole now comes with many modifications, including other vegetables, such as peas or edamame; dairy; and even chunks of fruit. Make this aromatic, herbaceous variation in the summer, when the herbs have reached their peak.

SERVES 4 TO 6

Prep Time: 10 MINUTES

Total Time: 15 MINUTES

1 lime

1 Serrano chile

15 fresh cilantro

8 fresh leaves basil

8 fresh leaves mint

8 fresh leaves tarragon

1 small white onion

4 ripe Hass avocados

1 teaspoon salt

1. Juice the lime.

2. Halve the chile and seed it. Thinly slice one half and, in a small bowl or molcajete (page 201), grind the other half into a paste.

3. Finely mince the cilantro, basil, mint, and tarragon and dice the onion.

4. Halve and pit the avocados and, still in the peel, slice the flesh into chunks.

5. In a medium bowl, mash the avocado chunks with a fork, leaving some chunks for texture.

6. Add the lime juice, onion, chile paste, and minced herbs and stir to combine.

7. Top with the sliced Serranos and serve.

Cilantro Lime Alioli

From the Latin phrase *alium et oleum,* aioli—which comes into English from Occitan, an ancient language spoken in southern France—and *alioli*, the Spanish version of the word, both mean "garlic and oil." A quick lesson on culinary vocab and history: Aioli consists of garlic emulsified in olive oil, sometimes with egg yolk, and comes from ancient Rome. In the first century AD, Pliny wrote about a difficult-to-emulsify sauce of oil, garlic, and salt. Alioli builds on that foundation with an acid, such as vinegar or lemon juice, added in Menorca (now part of Spain), possibly during the Renaissance. Mayonnaise contains egg yolks and oil not from olives and also comes from Menorca, specifically Mahón, the capital. In 1756, during the Seven Years' War, French forces laid siege to the British-controlled island. One version of the story holds that, because the island lacked cream, a French chef improvised a sauce from eggs and oil. This *salsa mahonesa* became mayonnaise (one of the mother sauces) in French and then English. The Spanish brought this trio of sauces to America. Recipes for salsa mahonesa appear in *Nuevo Cocinero Mejicano*, published in Paris in 1872, and in *La Cocinera Poblana*, published in Mexico in 1913. Alioli and mayonnaise occur widely in Latin American food: Mexican elote, Argentinian salsa golf (also called *salsa rosada* or mayochup), Cuban *arroz imperial*, Dominican ensalada rusa, and more. Chile ranks as the world's third-biggest market for mayonnaise and number one in Latin America. In the 1980s and '90s, Maricel Presilla, Cuban chef and author of *Gran Cocina Latina*, helped popularize pairing thinner French fry–sized fried yuca with a cilantro sauce at Victor's Café in New York City. It became the restaurant's most post popular appetizer, and its popularity grew when Victor's Café opened a location in Miami. The dish became ubiquitous in Cuban restaurants there, such as Versailles and La Carreta. This creamy dipping sauce features good tang and zest, making it perfect with Yuca Fries (page 65), Collard Greens Empanadas (page 66), and any other dish that calls for mayonnaise.

YIELDS APPROXIMATELY 1½ CUPS

Prep Time: 10 MINUTES

Total Time: 15 MINUTES

4 cloves garlic

½ teaspoon salt

2 egg yolks

1 cup Spanish extra-virgin olive oil

1½ tablespoons fresh lime juice

2 tablespoons chopped cilantro

1. Peel and mince the garlic.

2. In a molcajete (page 201), grind the garlic and salt until a paste forms. Set aside.

3. In the bowl of a stand mixer, whisk the egg yolks for 30 seconds. Add the garlic paste and whisk to combine.

4. Fit the stand mixer with the whisk attachment, place the bowl on the stand, set the speed to low, and mix for 10 minutes.

5. While the sauce is mixing, slowly add the olive oil.

6. After 8 or 9 minutes, add the lime juice.

7. When done mixing, add the cilantro and mix lightly with a spatula to incorporate.

NOTES

• The traditional method calls for emulsifying by hand, but there's no need to lose an arm if you have a stand mixer.

• The final texture should feel slightly thicker than mayonnaise.

• In an airtight container in the refrigerator, it will stay fresh for 5 to 7 days.

TIPS

• To make the garlic easier to grind, roast it first. Cook it in a 375°F oven for 30 minutes, until soft. Let it cool enough to handle, about 10 minutes.

• Add the olive oil *slowly*. Adding too much too quickly will cause the sauce to break, and you'll have to start over.

VARIATION

If you can't or don't eat eggs or want to try something like the ancient Roman version, omit the eggs and proceed with the recipe as written.

Corn Tortilla Chips

You could buy these from the store, but fresh tastes better. It's worth the extra effort and a few extra minutes.

SERVES 6
Prep Time: 5 MINUTES
Cook Time: 10 MINUTES
Total Time: 15 MINUTES

Canola or vegetable oil for frying
6 Corn Tortillas (page 210)
Salt

1. In a heavy-bottomed skillet over medium-high heat, heat 1 to 2 inches of oil to 375°F.

2. While the oil heats, stack the tortillas and use a pizza cutter to slice them into 36 equal wedges.

3. Working in small batches of roughly 6, fry the wedges until they lightly brown and crisp, about 1 minute, then flip and fry for 1 more minute.

4. Use a spider skimmer or slotted metal spoon to remove the chips from the oil and transfer to a paper towel–lined plate or baking sheet to cool and drain.

5. Season with salt to taste.

VARIATIONS

• For baked chips, preheat the oven to 350°F and line 2 baking sheets with foil. Lightly drizzle the wedges in oil and toss gently by hand or use a pastry brush to coat evenly, or spray them all on both sides with cooking spray. Place the raw chips on the prepared baking sheets without overlapping or crowding. Bake until golden, about 15 minutes, flipping them halfway through. Sprinkle with salt and let cool for 5 minutes before serving.

• Try these seasoning combinations for a new take on your chips. Mix the spices together, sprinkle over freshly made chips, and mix gently to coat. For dessert chips, use 1 tablespoon of ground cinnamon and 2 tablespoons of granulated sugar. For smoky chips, use 1 tablespoon each of cumin and smoked paprika and 1 teaspoon each of salt and freshly ground black pepper. For za'atar chips, use 2½ tablespoons of za'atar and 1 teaspoon of salt.

Doraditos

See page 56 for the origins of the Frito-Lay Corporation, which Archibald West joined in 1960 as VP of marketing. According to his daughter, the family was on vacation in San Diego the next year, and inspiration struck when he spotted people eating deep-fried corn chips at a roadside restaurant. The company debuted Doritos at the Casa de Fritos Restaurant in Disneyland in 1964. The product name elides the Spanish word *doraditos*, which means "little golden things," and Frito-Lay sold them nationwide two years later, making them America's first national tortilla chips. After West died in 2011, attendees at his funeral reportedly tossed in a Dorito while his ashes were being interred. This recipe is fun to make with kids and tastes just as good as—if not better than!—its store-bought sibling.

SERVES 6
Prep Time: 5 MINUTES
Cook Time: 10 MINUTES
Total Time: 15 MINUTES

6 ounces Corn Tortilla Chips (page 206)
1 tablespoon grated Parmesan cheese
¾ teaspoon chili powder
¾ teaspoon smoked paprika
¼ teaspoon garlic powder
¼ teaspoon onion powder
¼ teaspoon salt

1. While you fry the tortilla chips, assemble the seasoning blend: In a medium bowl, mix together the cheese, chili powder, paprika, garlic powder, onion powder, and salt.

2. Transfer the seasoning mixture to a spice/coffee grinder, mortar and pestle, or molcajete (page 201) and grind to a powder.

3. While the tortilla chips drain and cool, sprinkle them generously with the seasoning mixture.

NOTES
• Store leftover seasoning in an airtight container for future use.

• Store the chips in an airtight container for up to 2 weeks, but they taste so good that you probably will eat them all before then.

VARIATIONS
• To make ranch-style chips, add 2 ounces of dried ranch seasoning to the spice mixture.

• To season baked chips, place the ground spice mixture in a large resealable plastic storage bag. In batches, place the baked chips in the bag and shake to coat well. Remove from the bag and let them cool completely, for 1 to 2 hours, so they crisp.

Queso Blanco

In America, "queso" abbreviates *chile con queso*, a silky thick Tex-Mex Mornay sauce distinct from Mexican *queso fundido* ("melted cheese"). Queso fundido combines several white cheeses, usually Chihuahua and asadero, with chorizo and/or peppers and is served with tortillas, salsa, and pickled veggies. Fondue-like Tex-Mex queso melts one American-style yellow or white cheese and goes with crispy tortilla chips. As with many Tex-Mex foods, it likely originated in San Antonio in 1900, in this case from restaurateur Otis Fansworth. Another claim credits Miguel Martinez, who opened the Martinez Café (later called El Fenix) in Dallas in 1918. Whatever the origin, the popularity of queso surged along with the rise of processed foods and TV dinners in the 1960s and '70s. Identifiably Texan, it has become a mainstay at cookouts, sporting events, and any gathering that calls for tortilla chips.

SERVES 10
Prep Time: 5 MINUTES
Cook Time: 15 MINUTES
Total Time: 20 MINUTES

2 pounds Monterey Jack cheese, not shredded

One 12-ounce can evaporated milk

1 tablespoon cornstarch

One 4-ounce can green chiles, drained

1 teaspoon red pepper flakes

½ teaspoon chili powder

½ teaspoon ground cumin

¼ teaspoon salt

¼ teaspoon freshly ground black pepper

1. Grate or chop the cheese.

2. In a small saucepan over medium-high heat, whisk together the evaporated milk and cornstarch. As soon as the mixture simmers, immediately reduce the heat to low.

3. Add ½ cup of the cheese, increase the heat to medium-low, and whisk constantly to melt and combine. When the cheese completely incorporates, stir in the remaining cheese, ½ cup at a time, whisking constantly and waiting until each portion melts and incorporates completely before adding the next.

4. Add the chiles, red pepper flakes, chili powder, cumin, salt, and black pepper and stir to combine. Serve warm.

NOTE
To make a smooth sauce, you need to start with a roux, so don't jump the gun and add the cheese along with cornstarch. If you do, it will clump. Some cheeses don't melt well together, so use just one variety rather than a mixture. Adding the cheese a little bit at a time also helps avoid clumps. Don't dump it all in, stir the sin out of it, and expect smooth sauce. Don't overcook the cheese or let it boil, either, lest the oils separate and result in a grainy mess.

Cilantro Lime Rice

Growing up in Panama, Hawaii, and Japan, I ate rice every. single. day. Before shipping me off to college, my mother gave me a small rice cooker just in case the dining halls didn't serve rice or, if they did, it tasted terrible. Simply cooked white rice delights me—and simple doesn't mean flavorless—but I also adore cilantro lime rice. The coriander plant, from which cilantro (the leaves) comes, originated in prehistory, probably around the Mediterranean. Don't confuse it with culantro (Mexican coriander), native to Central and South America. Like many ingredients, the Spanish introduced coriander to the Western Hemisphere in the 1500s. Unlike other Latin American countries, Mexico doesn't consume a lot of rice, but South Carolina and Georgia grew *tons* of it from the colonial period through Reconstruction. Texas started growing it commercially in 1853 and California in 1912. All of which makes cilantro rice distinctly American Latino. Mexican Americans in Texas and California likely added cilantro to white rice, which Tex-Mex and Cal-Mex cuisines adopted and Chipotle popularized. Put this rice in burritos, pair it with Refried Beans (page 230) or meat, or enjoy it on its own.

SERVES 6
Prep Time: 10 MINUTES
Cook Time: 20 MINUTES
Total Time: 30 MINUTES

2 cups water
1 tablespoon canola oil
½ teaspoon kosher salt
1 cup uncooked long-grain white rice
2 bay leaves
2 limes
¼ cup chopped fresh cilantro

1. In a medium lidded saucepan over high heat, bring the water, canola oil, and kosher salt to a boil.

2. While the water heats, rinse the rice in cold water until it runs clear.

3. When the saucepan water is boiling, add the rinsed rice and bay leaves and stir. Cover the saucepan, lower the heat to low, and simmer until the rice becomes tender, 15 to 17 minutes. If any liquid remains, cover again and cook for a few more minutes until it absorbs.

4. Meanwhile, juice the limes.

5. When the rice has finished cooking, turn off the heat and let stand, covered, for 2 minutes.

6. Fluff the rice with a fork, add the cilantro and lime juice, and stir to combine.

Corn Tortillas

Before recorded history, corn tortillas originated in what is Mexico today. They remain one of the only purely Indigenous dishes in American Latino cuisines. See page 10 for more about the nixtamalization process that creates masa harina.

YIELDS 12 TO 16 TORTILLAS
Prep Time: 15 MINUTES
Cook Time: 15 MINUTES
Total Time: 30 MINUTES

1 pound masa harina (instant corn flour)
1 to 1½ teaspoons salt (optional)
2 cups water

NOTE

The dough balls dry out quickly, so press them immediately.

TIP

For Steps 3 and 4, here's an easy way to create dough balls of equal size: Roll the dough into a log about 1½ inches in diameter. Slice it into 16 disks, each about ½ inch thick, and roll the disks into balls.

1. In a large bowl, combine the masa harina and salt (if using) and slowly pour in the water.

2. Using your hands or a stand mixer fitted with a dough hook, knead the dough until the water incorporates completely, leaving no dry or powdery spots. It should feel moist but not sticky.

3. Pinch off a piece of dough and roll it with your hands into a ball the size of a plum or large golf ball.

4. Repeat with the remaining dough. You should have 12 to 16 balls.

5. Flatten the dough balls with a tortillera (page 211) or a heavy round pot.

6. With a tortillera: Lay a square piece of plastic wrap or parchment paper on the bottom of the tortillera. Place a dough ball in the center. Place another piece of plastic wrap or parchment paper on top. Squeeze the handle to close the machine and press the dough to about 6 inches in diameter.

7. With a heavy round pot: On a flat surface, lay a square piece of plastic wrap or parchment paper. Place a dough ball in the center. Place another piece of plastic wrap or parchment paper on top. Place the heavy pot on top and press it down until the dough reaches about 6 inches in diameter.

8. To cook, gently peel the plastic wrap or parchment paper from a tortilla.

9. Heat a comal, griddle, or cast-iron skillet over medium-high heat. Cook the tortilla until it puffs slightly and toasts lightly, 30 seconds to 1 minute on each side.

10. Repeat, one by one, with the remaining raw tortillas. Serve immediately or let cool to room temperature and store in a resealable plastic storage bag.

Rainbow Tortillas

Use different shades of masa harina—white, red, yellow, and blue—to create rainbow tortillas. Mix the separate doughs together before pressing to make showstopping, psychedelic tortillas.

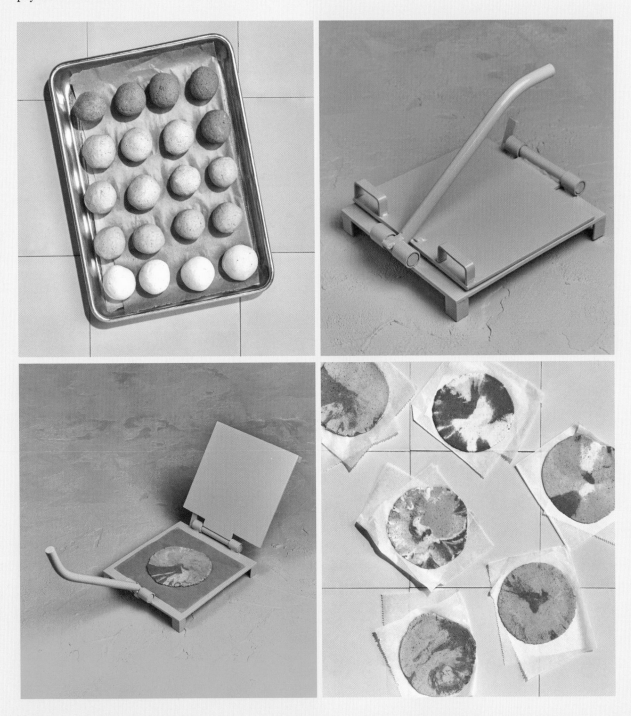

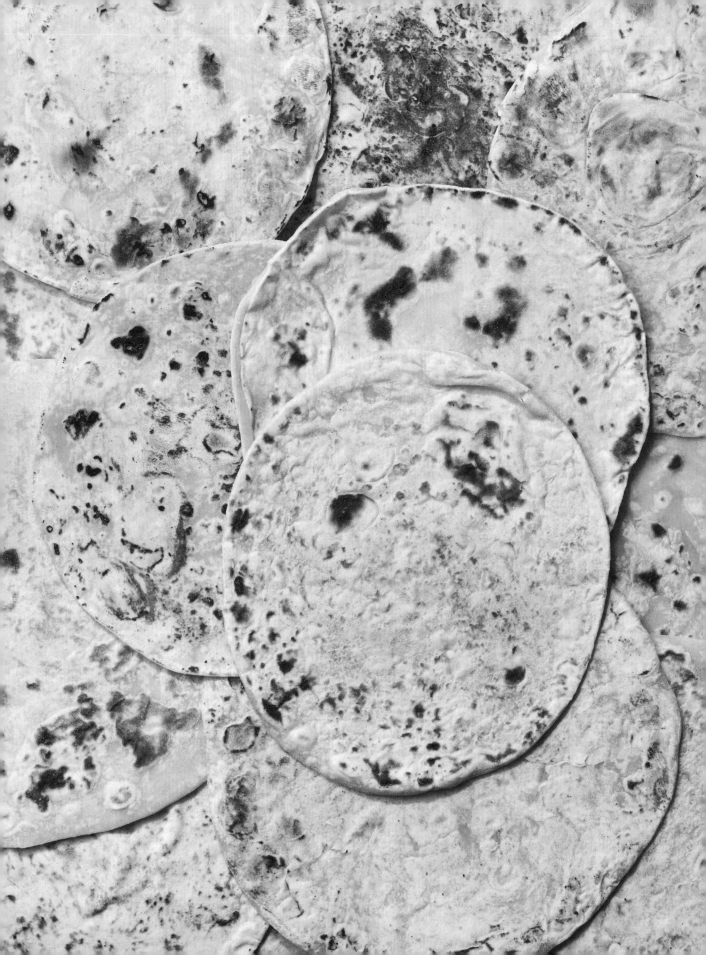

Flour Tortillas

In Spanish, *tortilla* means "little cake" (not to be confused with *tortilla española*, which Americans would identify as an omelet). Flour tortillas originated in Spain during the Muslim occupation, and we have complete recipes for them from the 1200s. During colonization, the Spanish brought wheat and flour tortillas to the Western Hemisphere, where the grain favors highland growing conditions. As a result, flour tortillas generally appear only in the cuisines of northern Mexico and the American Southwest, where of course they play an integral role in Tex-Mex foods. Sonoran flour tortillas, containing lard instead of butter, stretch paper thin and cook on a griddle that creates small blisters with a slightly smoky flavor. That style instantly became American when the country of Texas joined the Union in 1845 and, after the Mexican-American War ended in 1848, the Mexican Cession transferred parts of what became New Mexico, Colorado, and Wyoming; most of Arizona; and all of Nevada and California to the United States. Some people wrongly disdain the flour tortilla as inauthentic, but plenty more people love it, including me. Numerous recipes in this book call for using these buttery, rich tortillas, but you can eat them plain, with a Mojito Iced Coffee (page 188) or Tres Leches Latte (page 191), for a light breakfast or snack.

YIELDS 24 TORTILLAS
Prep Time: 20 MINUTES
Cook Time: 10 MINUTES
Total Time: 30 MINUTES

4 cups all-purpose flour, plus more
    for dusting
2 teaspoons salt
8 tablespoons (1 stick) unsalted butter,
    at room temperature, plus more
    for shaping
1¼ cups warm water, plus more if
    needed (110°F to 115°F)

1. In a large bowl, stir together the flour and salt.

2. With your hands or a pastry cutter, cut the butter into the flour mixture until it achieves a crumbly texture.

3. Gradually add the 1¼ cups of warm water to the flour mixture and mix until a dough forms and becomes sticky. If it's too dry, add a little more water.

4. On a flat, lightly floured surface, knead the dough until soft and smooth, about 5 minutes.

5. Divide the dough into 8 equal portions.

6. Lightly butter your hands, roll each portion into a ball, and place the balls on a plate. As you make them, cover the balls with plastic wrap so they don't dry out.

7. Remove the plastic wrap, cover with a clean kitchen towel, and let rest for 15 minutes.

8. Place a comal, griddle pan, or cast-iron skillet over medium heat.

CONTINUES $\longrightarrow$

9. While the pan heats, flatten the dough with a large tortillera (page 211) or by hand.

10. With a tortillera: Lay a square piece of plastic wrap or parchment paper on the bottom of the tortillera. Place a dough ball in the center. Place another piece of plastic wrap or parchment paper on top. Squeeze the handle to close the machine and press the dough to about ⅛ inch thick and 10 to 12 inches in diameter.

11. By hand: Lightly sprinkle a clean flat surface with all-purpose flour. Using a rolling pin, roll the dough—back and forth, side to side, flipping occasionally—to about ⅛ inch thick and 10 to 12 inches in diameter.

12. Gently place a raw tortilla in the heated pan. Cook until it begins to bubble and blister, about 30 seconds, then flip and cook for 30 more seconds.

13. Place the cooked tortillas in a tortilla warmer (tortillero) or between clean kitchen towels while cooking the remaining tortillas.

Salsa Roja

This red chile sauce goes perfectly with burritos, enchiladas, stewing meats, tamales, and more. Smother basically anything you like with it. This recipe uses red New Mexico chiles, but you can substitute ancho or other red chiles.

YIELDS APPROXIMATELY 2 CUPS
Prep Time: 5 MINUTES
Cook Time: 30 MINUTES
Total Time: 35 MINUTES

10 to 20 dried red New Mexico chiles
¼ medium yellow or white onion
2 cups unsalted chicken broth
3 cloves garlic
½ teaspoon dried Mexican oregano
½ teaspoon toasted and ground cumin
¼ teaspoon salt, plus more to taste

1. Preheat the oven to 250°F and line a baking sheet with aluminum foil.

2. On the prepared baking sheet, place the chiles in a single layer, bake for 10 minutes, flip the chiles over, and bake for 10 more minutes.

3. Remove from the oven, let the chiles cool enough to handle, then remove the stems and seeds.

4. In a large lidded pot over high heat, cover the chiles and onion with water, bring the water to a boil, lower the heat to low, cover, and simmer for 10 minutes.

5. Transfer the boiled chiles and onion to a blender. Add the chicken broth, garlic, Mexican oregano, cumin, and salt. Blend until smooth.

6. Strain the salsa through a fine-mesh sieve and adjust the salt to taste.

Mexican Rice

Arroz a la Mexicana, arroz mexicano, arroz rojo, or just red rice. The color comes from the tomatoes and the achiote in the sazón. If you like Charleston red rice or Gullah rice, give this Tex-Mex version a taste.

SERVES 4
Prep Time: 5 MINUTES
Cook Time: 40 MINUTES
Total Time: 45 MINUTES

1 cup uncooked long-grain rice

2 tablespoons vegetable or canola oil

½ teaspoon minced garlic

½ teaspoon salt

½ teaspoon cumin, Sazón (page 197), or Taco Seasoning (page 198)

¼ medium yellow or white onion

2 cups chicken broth

4 ounces tomato sauce, or 1 tablespoon tomato paste

3 to 6 sprigs cilantro

1. Rinse and drain the rice.

2. In a large lidded saucepan over medium heat, cook the oil, rinsed rice, garlic, salt, and cumin, stirring constantly, until the rice puffs and turns golden, about 5 minutes.

3. Meanwhile, chop the onion.

4. Add the onion and cook until softened, 5 to 7 minutes.

5. Add the chicken broth and tomato sauce and bring to a boil.

6. Lower the heat to low, add the cilantro, cover, and simmer for 20 to 25 minutes.

7. Fluff the rice with a fork and serve.

Pão de Queijo

In the mid-1900s, gauchos (cowboys) of southern Brazil pioneered churrasco. At large gatherings, they roasted salted, skewered beef over embers, slicing individual servings for their guests, as Brazilians still do today. In 1979, Fogo de Chão opened in Porto Alegre, the capital of Rio Grande do Sul State, Brazil, and came stateside in 1997. The next year, in the same suburb of Dallas as the first Fogo de Chão in the United States, Texas de Brazil opened its first location. Two cowboy cultures with a passion for meat collided perfectly and became a sensation. Since then, *churrascarias* (Brazilian steakhouses) have become a popular destination for date nights and guys' nights out. One of the best churrascaria offerings is this Brazilian cheese bread made from native cassava. Neighboring Argentina and Paraguay also claim credit for the gluten-free snack, called chipá in those two countries, but it ultimately came from the Indigenous Guarani people, who live in an area common to all three nations. Enjoy it with steak, at your next barbecue, or even with coffee for breakfast.

SERVES 12 TO 18
Prep Time: 20 MINUTES
Cook Time: 25 MINUTES
Total Time: 45 MINUTES

⅓ cup unsalted butter, melted
½ cup whole milk
1 teaspoon salt
⅓ cup water
2 cups tapioca flour
2 large eggs, at room temperature
1 cup freshly grated Parmesan cheese

TIP

To help add the tapioca flour immediately yet gradually in Step 3, place it in the center of a piece of parchment paper, carefully bring the sides together, and slowly funnel the flour into the saucepan.

1. Preheat the oven to 450°F.

2. In a large saucepan over high heat, combine the butter, milk, salt, and water. Bring to a boil, then immediately remove from the heat.

3. Immediately yet gradually whisk the tapioca flour into the mixture until smooth. Let it cool for 10 to 15 minutes.

4. While the tapioca roux cools, beat the eggs in a small bowl and line a baking sheet with parchment paper.

5. Stir the eggs and Parmesan into the tapioca mixture until well combined. The resulting dough will look chunky, like cottage cheese.

6. Scoop a heaping tablespoon of dough. With lightly wet hands, roll it into a ball and place it on the prepared baking sheet.

7. Repeat with the remaining dough, placing the balls about 1 inch apart on the baking sheet.

8. Bake for 5 minutes, lower the heat to 400°F, and bake until the balls turn golden, 15 to 20 more minutes, making sure not to burn the bottoms. Serve warm.

CONTINUES ⟶

VARIATIONS

• If you prefer, for Steps 4 and 5, you can transfer the roux to the bowl of a stand mixer fitted with a paddle attachment or use a hand mixer and mix on low for 1 minute to release steam. Then add half of the beaten eggs at a time, followed by the cheese, and mix for 30 seconds.

• Instead of Parmesan, try freshly grated mozzarella, feta, or your cheese of choice.

• Try adding garlic or parsley to the dough if you like.

• You also can prepare this dish with a regular or mini muffin tin. Increase the milk to ⅔ cup, reduce the tapioca flour to 1½ cups and the cheese to ½ cup (packed), and use 1 large egg. Spray a standard 12-well nonstick or silicone muffin pan with cooking spray and process all the ingredients in a food processor until smooth. Divide the batter equally among the prepared wells of the tin. Bake at 400°F until puffy and golden brown, 15 to 20 minutes. Let the tin cool on a wire rack for 5 minutes, plate the rolls, and serve warm.

Mofongo Mashed Potatoes

The word *mofongo* derives from the phrase *mfwenge-mfwenge*, which means "a great amount" in the Kongo language of West Africa. The origins of the dish begin with *fufu*, a pounded combination of boiled cassava, plantains, and malangas from Ghana, also in West Africa, which came to the Western Hemisphere with the Spanish slave trade. In the Caribbean, fufu took on elements of Indigenous and Spanish cuisines and evolved. The first recipe for mofongo appeared in *El Cocinero Puerto-Riqueño o Formulario*, Puerto Rico's first cookbook, published in 1859. Over the decades, the underlying recipe has changed, and this dish doesn't riff on it; rather, it hybridizes it with mashed potatoes. The buttery richness of the potatoes pairs perfectly with the slight sweetness of the plantains, and every bite bursts with garlicky flavor. This recipe works well for potato-heavy holidays, including Thanksgiving and Christmas, but it suits any occasion that calls for mashed potatoes, such as barbecues, cookouts, picnics, and more.

SERVES 4 TO 6

Prep Time: 5 MINUTES
Cook Time: 1 HOUR 10 MINUTES
Total Time: 1 HOUR 15 MINUTES

2 pounds medium Yukon Gold or Honey Gold potatoes (about 5)

Canola, corn, or vegetable oil for frying

3 ripe plantains (about 1¼ pounds)

4 to 5 cloves garlic

4 tablespoons (½ stick) unsalted butter

1 cup heavy cream or half-and-half, plus more as needed

1 teaspoon kosher salt, plus more as needed

4 ounces pork rinds or cracklings

Freshly ground black pepper

Coarsely chopped fresh cilantro leaves and tender stems for garnish

1. In a medium pot over medium-high heat, cover the potatoes with cold water by 1 inch. Bring to a boil, lower the heat to low, and simmer until the potatoes become fork-tender, 35 to 40 minutes.

2. Meanwhile, in a large saucepan over medium-high heat, heat 2 inches of oil (4 to 6 cups) to 350°F.

3. While the oil heats, peel the plantains and slice them crosswise into 1-inch-thick chunks.

4. Add half of the plantains to the oil and fry them until they turn golden brown and fork-tender, 5 to 7 minutes. Transfer them to a paper towel–lined plate to drain and cool.

5. Repeat Step 4 with the remaining plantains. Reserve the frying oil.

6. Mince the garlic.

7. In a small saucepan over low heat, add the butter and half of the garlic and cook until the butter melts and the garlic becomes fragrant but doesn't brown, about 5 minutes.

8. To the garlic-butter mixture, add the cream and ½ teaspoon of the salt. Increase the heat to medium and cook, stirring to combine, for 3 to 5 minutes. Remove from the heat.

CONTINUES $\longrightarrow$

9. When the potatoes have cooked, drain and return them to the pot, add the cream mixture, and use a masher to mash them until mostly smooth.

10. In a small skillet over medium heat, heat 2 teaspoons of the reserved plantain frying oil until it shimmers. Add the remaining half of the garlic and cook until fragrant, 1 to 2 minutes. Transfer the fried garlic and oil to a medium bowl.

11. Working in batches, add the plantains to the garlic oil and use a masher to mash them until mostly smooth. Stir to combine.

12. With your hands, crush the pork rinds into rough pieces. Add most of them to the plantains and stir to combine.

13. Add the plantain mixture to the potato mixture, add the remaining ½ teaspoon of salt, and stir to combine. Taste and season as needed with more salt and/or pepper.

14. Garnish with the remaining pork rinds and chopped cilantro.

Louisiana Hot Sauce

Indigenous peoples of the Western Hemisphere cooked with chile peppers for thousands of years before Europeans arrived, but the first mass-produced hot sauces hit the American market in the 1800s. Edmund McIlhenny created the most popular one, Tabasco pepper sauce, on Avery Island, south of Lafayette, Louisiana, in 1868. He called it Tabasco, after the Mexican state where the smoky pepper of the same name grows, which in turn comes from the Nahuatl word *tlapalco*, meaning "damp earth" or "humid land." This hot sauce lets the peppers do the talking. It leans heavy on the vinegar and light on the spice. Mexican hot sauces generally contain more spices.

YIELDS 2⅔ TO 3 CUPS
Prep Time: 5 MINUTES
Cook Time: 10 MINUTES, PLUS COOLING TIME
Total Time: 1 HOUR 20 MINUTES

1 pound fresh red Jalapeño, Tabasco, or chile peppers of choice
2 cups white vinegar
2 teaspoons salt
½ teaspoon granulated sugar

1. Stem the peppers.

2. In a large pot over high heat, combine the vinegar, peppers, and salt. Bring to a boil, lower the heat to medium, and simmer until the chiles soften, about 5 minutes.

3. Remove from the heat and let cool for 5 to 10 minutes.

4. Transfer the mixture to a blender or food processor and add the sugar. Blend or process until smooth. Let cool to room temperature, 40 minutes to 1 hour.

NOTES

• You can use the hot sauce as soon as it cools, but it tastes best after resting in the refrigerator for 2 weeks.

• In an airtight container, it will keep in the fridge for 4 months.

VARIATION

Instead of white vinegar, you can use apple cider vinegar or white wine vinegar.

Salsa Verde

Serve this green chile sauce with tortilla chips, over rice, on chilaquiles (page 24) or migas (page 16), as a dipping sauce, or as an accompaniment to any dish that needs some heat and acid.

YIELDS APPROXIMATELY 2⅔ CUPS
Prep Time: 5 MINUTES
Cook Time: 1 HOUR 5 MINUTES, PLUS SWEATING TIME
Total Time: 1 HOUR 35 MINUTES

1 pound tomatillos

3 or 4 green Serrano chile peppers

1 medium white onion

6 green New Mexico, Anaheim, or Poblano chile peppers

1 tablespoon vegetable oil

3 cloves garlic

2 to 3 sprigs epazote (optional)

1 cup fresh cilantro

1½ teaspoons salt or 1 cup vegetable broth

½ cup water, plus more if needed

1 tablespoon fresh lime juice

Additional salt to season

NOTE

Refrigerating the boiled vegetables helps prevent bitterness, so don't skip that part of Step 4!

VARIATION

Instead of salt or veggie broth, you can use one chicken bouillon cube or 1 cup of chicken broth.

1. Husk and rinse the tomatillos, stem and seed the Serranos, and halve the onion. Quarter one of the onion halves and slice the other.

2. In a large pot over medium-high heat, cover the tomatillos, Serranos, and the quartered onion half with water.

3. Bring the water to a boil, lower the heat to low, and cook until the vegetables soften, about 20 minutes. Don't overboil or the tomatillos will burst. Their color will change from bright to pale green.

4. Drain the boiled vegetables, let cool to room temperature, and refrigerate for 10 to 15 minutes.

5. While the boiled vegetables cool, preheat the oven to 450°F.

6. Place the green chile peppers on an unlined baking sheet and roast in the oven until they char and blister, 25 to 40 minutes.

7. Transfer the roasted peppers to a bowl and covered with foil or to a resealable plastic storage bag. Let the peppers sweat for 20 minutes.

8. While the peppers sweat, prepare the rest of the vegetables: In a skillet over medium heat, heat the oil and cook 2 of the garlic cloves, the sliced onion half, and the epazote (if using) until the garlic becomes golden and fragrant and the onion softens and is turning translucent but hasn't browned, 3 to 5 minutes.

9. Remove the charred skin and seeds from the roasted peppers.

10. Remove the chilled vegetables from the fridge and place them in a blender.

11. Rinse the cilantro and add it to the blender, followed by the remaining garlic clove, the fried garlic mixture, the roasted peppers, the salt or broth, and the water. Blend until smooth. If the sauce is too thick, add more water, 1 tablespoon at a time, and blend.

12. Let cool to room temperature and refrigerate.

13. When ready to serve, add the lime juice, stir to combine, and salt to taste.

Empanada Disks

If you can make tortillas, you can make empanada dough. The fat in this dough makes it taste rich, but you can modify it however you like. The world is your, well, empanada.

YIELDS 12 EMPANADA DISKS
Prep Time: 1 HOUR 10 MINUTES
Active Time: 1 HOUR
Total Time: 2 HOURS 10 MINUTES

3 cups all-purpose flour

½ teaspoon salt

1 teaspoon baking powder

½ cup lard, 8 tablespoons (1 stick) unsalted butter, or ½ cup vegetable shortening, cold

1 cup water

1 teaspoon vegetable or canola oil

VARIATIONS

• Make it vegetarian or vegan by selecting the appropriate fat.

• For a nice hit of acid, swap out 1 tablespoon of the water for the same amount of fresh lemon juice, or ¼ cup of the water for the same amount of orange juice.

• For dessert empanadas, add 1 tablespoon of granulated sugar to the dry flour mixture.

1. In a food processor, pulse the flour, salt, baking powder, and lard until mixed.

2. Add the water, ½ cup at a time, and pulse until clumps begin to form.

3. Remove the dough from the food processor, shape into a ball, and knead lightly for about 1 minute.

4. Lightly coat the dough ball with oil and place in a bowl. Loosely cover the bowl with plastic wrap and let the dough rest at room temperature for 1 hour.

5. Divide the dough into 12 equal portions and roll each by hand into a ball.

6. Flatten the dough balls with a tortillera (page 211) or by hand.

7. With a tortillera: Lay a square piece of plastic wrap or parchment paper on the bottom of the tortillera. Place a dough ball in the center. Place another piece of plastic wrap or parchment paper on top. Squeeze the handle to close the machine and press the dough to about ¼ inch thick and 5 to 6 inches in diameter.

8. By hand: Lightly sprinkle a clean flat surface with all-purpose flour. Using a rolling pin, roll the dough—back and forth, side to side, flipping occasionally—to about ¼ inch thick and 5 to 6 inches in diameter.

9. Evenly space the disks in a single layer on 1 or 2 ungreased baking sheets or stack them on a baking sheet with squares of parchment paper between the disks.

10. Chill for 30 minutes to 1 hour prior to baking or frying.

Dulce de Leche

This thick, creamy sauce inspires such ardent passion among its devotees that numerous countries claim credit for its origins. A heated battle continues to rage among Argentina, Chile, Colombia, Peru, and Uruguay. One of the many creation stories centers on a maid working for Juan Ortiz de Rozas y López de Osornio, a 19th-century Argentinean politician. She was cooking milk and sugar, stepped away for a moment, and forgot about the pot, which resulted in the sweet treat. Forgetfulness can be a beautiful thing. Because it must contain milk, dulce de leche isn't caramel, which comes from caramelizing sugar in water. Mexican *cajeta* uses goat's milk, whereas dulce de leche calls for cow's milk. You can buy it from the store, but where's the fun in that? Make it yourself and slather it on *everything*.

YIELDS 1½ CUPS
Prep Time: 5 MINUTES
Cook Time: 2 HOURS 35 MINUTES
Total Time: 2 HOURS 40 MINUTES

4 cups whole milk
1 cup granulated sugar
¼ teaspoon baking soda
2 tablespoons water
2 tablespoons unsalted butter, at room temperature
1 teaspoon vanilla extract

NOTES

• Dulce de leche will stay fresh in the fridge for up to 2 weeks.

• To thin it, add a couple of tablespoons of water or milk and stir to combine. If you're feeling more ambitious, use a double boiler or set a heatproof glass or stainless steel bowl atop a pot filled with a few inches of water. Bring the water to a boil, then lower the heat to low. Stir the desired amount of dulce de leche in the top of the double boiler or in the bowl until it warms and loosens to the desired viscosity.

1. In a small saucepan over medium heat, bring the milk to a boil. Immediately lower the heat to low and simmer, stirring every 3 to 5 minutes.

2. After about 30 minutes, add the sugar and continue to simmer and stir until the sugar dissolves fully, 3 to 5 minutes.

3. In a small glass or dish, whisk together the baking soda and water and add to the milk.

4. Continue to simmer, stirring, for 1 hour.

5. Add the butter and vanilla and (you guessed it) keep stirring, about 1 more hour.

6. When the milk has caramelized, thickened, and reduced to 1½ cups, remove it from the heat.

7. Let it thicken in the pan for 10 to 15 minutes.

8. Transfer to an airtight glass container and let it cool to room temperature.

VARIATION

Here's a crazy easy hack for making your own dulce de leche at home: Remove the label from a 14-ounce can of sweetened condensed milk. In a large pot over medium-high heat, cover the can with water by at least 3 inches. Bring the water to a boil, lower the heat to medium-low, and simmer for 3 hours, rotating the can every 30 minutes. If the water level runs low, add more so that the can stays covered. Turn off the heat and let the can cool in the water for 1 hour. When the water and can have reached room temperature, open the can, spoon or pour the dulce de leche into a small bowl, and stir to combine.

Refried Beans

Last but certainly not least comes this cornerstone of Tex-Mex cuisine. About a century ago, this dish of seasoned beans cooked low and slow originated in northern Mexico before crossing the border to Texas, which heartily adopted it. Most recipes call for pinto beans, which result in an extra-creamy texture, but some use black beans, which taste earthier. Also, the beans aren't fried twice, they're cooked twice. Now you know. If you eat this dish on its own, rather than making it as part of another recipe, serve it with Cotija cheese, lime juice, and fresh cilantro to taste.

SERVES 6 TO 8
Prep Time: 8 HOURS
Cook Time: 1 HOUR 35 MINUTES
Total Time: 9 HOURS 35 MINUTES

1 pound dried pinto beans
    (about 2 cups)
½ to 1 large white or yellow onion
2 to 3 cloves garlic
2 teaspoons salt, or more to taste
2 to 3 tablespoons lard, vegetable
    shortening, or oil
¾ teaspoon toasted and ground cumin
½ teaspoon dried Mexican oregano

1. Sort and rinse the beans.

2. In a large lidded pot, cover the beans with water and soak, covered, overnight.

3. Drain the beans, return them to the pot over medium-high heat, and cover them with fresh water by 2 inches.

4. Quarter the onion, mince the garlic, and add both and the salt to the pot.

5. Bring the water to a boil, lower the heat to low, cover, and simmer for 1 hour, stirring occasionally. If, after 1 hour, the beans haven't cooked completely, let them simmer for a few more minutes until done.

6. Drain the beans, reserving the bean broth, onion, and garlic.

7. In a large skillet over medium heat, heat the lard.

8. While the fat heats, use paper towels to pat the onion and garlic dry and then chop them.

9. Add the onion and garlic to the skillet and cook, stirring occasionally, until they soften and become fragrant, 3 to 5 minutes.

10. Add the beans, cumin, oregano, and ¼ cup of bean broth and cook for 30 minutes, stirring occasionally. If, after 30 minutes, the beans haven't cooked completely, continue to cook for 15 to 30 minutes, until they soften and become fork-tender.

TIP

In Step 5, check for doneness by pressing 1 or 2 beans against the side of the pot with a fork. They should be plump and mash easily but not be mushy. Save the leftover bean broth to stir into any leftovers that dry out. As they chill in the refrigerator, they'll thicken.

11. For a chunkier consistency, use a fork or masher to mash the beans. For a smooth texture, remove the beans from the heat, allow them to cool for 5 to 10 minutes, transfer them to a food processor, add a little bean broth, and process until smooth. For thicker consistency, use less bean broth; for thinner consistency, use more. If the beans dry out, add 1 tablespoon of bean broth at a time and stir until they rehydrate.

VARIATIONS

• Everyone has different preferences, so adjust the ingredients, including the cumin, to taste.

• To save time, buy three 15-ounce cans of cooked pinto beans and start at Step 3.

Acknowledgments

Thanks to—

Stacey Glick, my agent, for championing this book, and to Kate Heddings, for your kindness and instantly seeing this book for what it is.

Recipe testers Andrew Carr, David Fulbrook, Liz Provencher, Chelsie Pietras, Tommy Duong, Claire Matern, Danielle Sweet, Desiree Currie, Emily Saladino, Genevieve Montinar, Jon Goldberg, Joseph Puente, Laura Ratliff, Melissa Mesulam, Miriam Vaught, Pamela Smith, Rebecca Roland, Reema Desai, Sara Hundt, Tessa Flack, Tracy Wilk, and Yoriko Nakamura; and Thiago Pinheiro Jeronimo, for help with Portuguese translations.

The Countryman Press team, especially James Jayo, my editor, for seeing, believing, and accepting this book; for your thoughtful edits; and for always making my work better. Thank you for pushing me. I couldn't have done this without you, and I'm so proud of what we have done.

The photo shoot crew: food stylist César Aldrete, photographer Hipolito Torres, kitchen assistants Carolina Zapata and Madeline Muzzi, prop stylist Sean Dooley, production assistant Lemon Dierks, and Brandon Cruz of Summit68 Studios. *Muchas gracias* for helping my book come to delicious life.

Syma and Michelle. To my friends, who I feel so blessed that there might be too many to list, Jason Smart, the Basement Buddies, Ping Pong Crew, and family, Tía Silvia, cousin Bella, and Toby Kaplan for encouraging me to invest in myself.

JL, for believing in me and supporting me at the beginning of this crazy life. I think I finally can take off this necklace. I will treasure our friendship and what it means to me always.

Everyone who believed in me and helped me get to this place, no matter how long or briefly we may have known each other, thank you. Everyone who ever has felt *ni de aquí, ni de allá*—not from here, not from there—I hope this book helps you see that this is your place. Celebrate that. You who picked up this book, thank you for giving my words and recipes a chance.

Index

Page numbers in *italics* indicate illustrations.

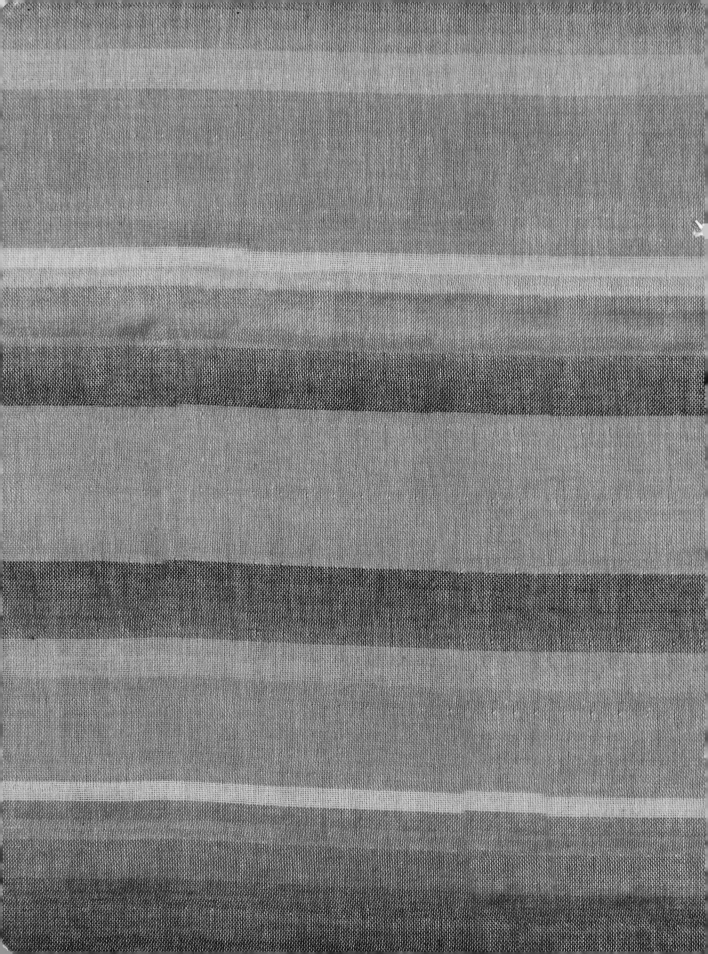